BWO

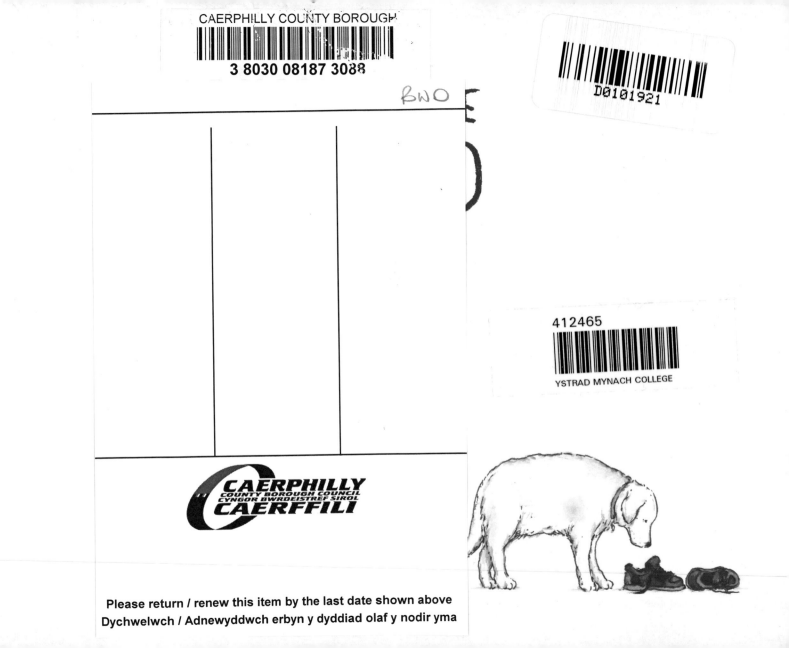

CAERPHILLY
COUNTY BOROUGH COUNCIL
CYNGOR BWRDEISTREF SIROL
CAERFFILI

Please return / renew this item by the last date shown above
Dychwelwch / Adnewyddwch erbyn y dyddiad olaf y nodir yma

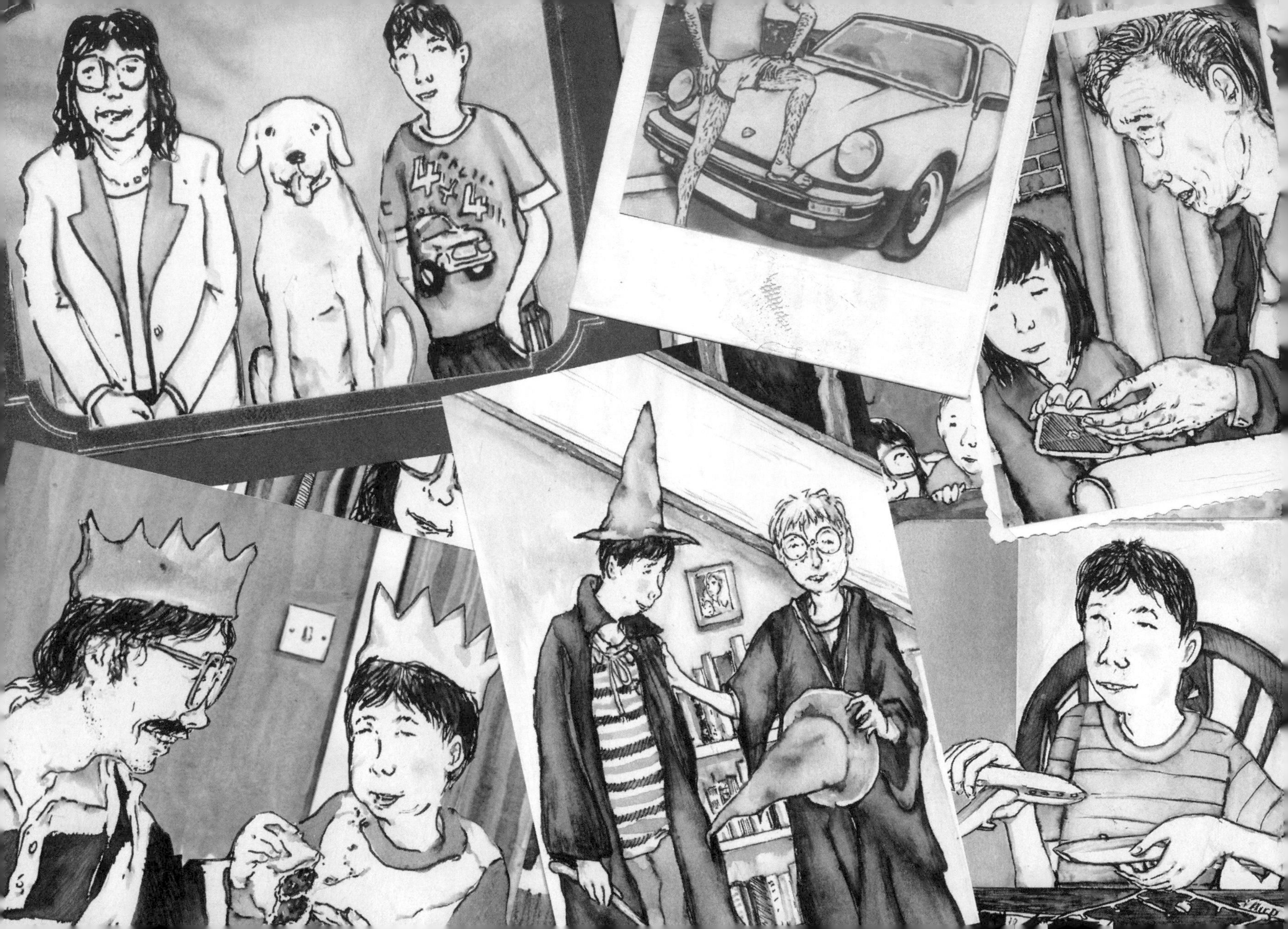

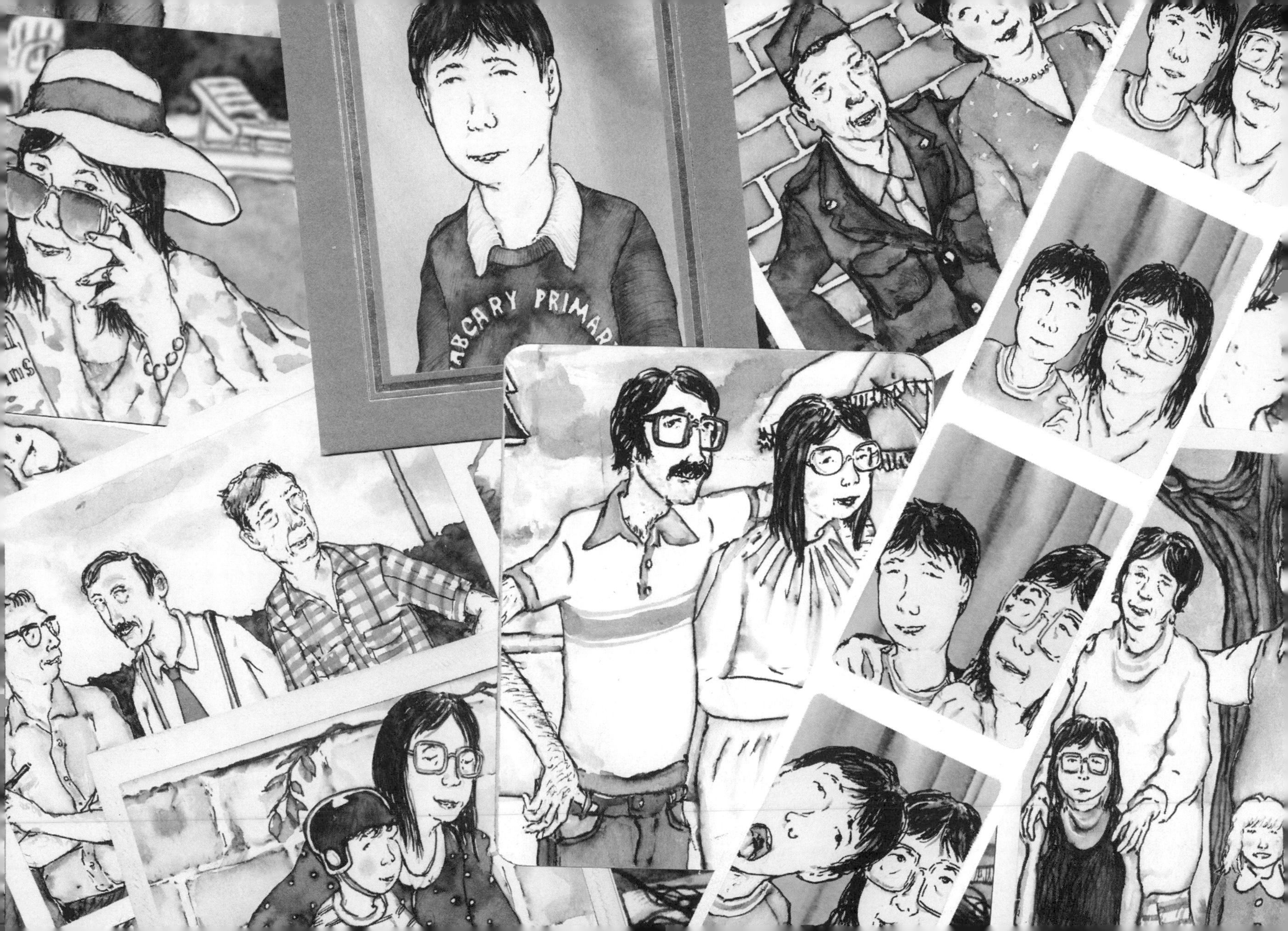
ABCARY PRIMAR

DAYS OF THE BAGNOLD SUMMER

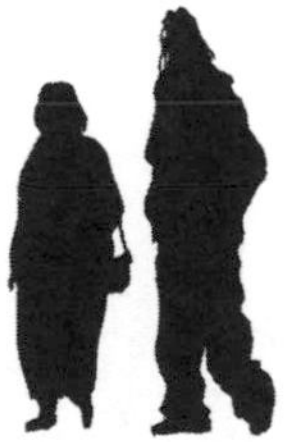

JOFF WINTERHART

JONATHAN CAPE
LONDON

PUBLISHED BY JONATHAN CAPE 2012 10 9 8 7 6 5 4 3 2 1
COPYRIGHT © JOFF WINTERHART 2012

FIRST PUBLISHED IN GREAT BRITAIN IN 2012 BY JONATHAN CAPE
RANDOM HOUSE, 20 VAUXHALL BRIDGE ROAD,
LONDON SW1V 2SA
www.capegraphicnovels.co.uk

ADDRESSES FOR COMPANIES WITHIN THE RANDOM HOUSE GROUP LIMITED CAN BE FOUND AT:
www.randomhouse.co.uk/offices.htm
THE RANDOM HOUSE GROUP LIMITED REG. NO. 954009
A CIP CATALOGUE RECORD FOR THIS BOOK IS AVAILABLE FROM THE BRITISH LIBRARY
ISBN 9780224090841
THE RANDOM HOUSE GROUP LIMITED SUPPORTS THE FOREST STEWARDSHIP COUNCIL (FSC®), THE LEADING INTERNATIONAL FOREST CERTIFICATION ORGANISATION. OUR BOOKS CARRYING THE FSC LABEL ARE PRINTED ON FSC® CERTIFIED PAPER. FSC IS THE ONLY FOREST CERTIFICATION SCHEME ENDORSED BY THE LEADING ENVIRONMENTAL ORGANISATIONS, INCLUDING GREENPEACE. OUR PAPER PROCUREMENT POLICY CAN BE FOUND AT www.randomhouse.co.uk/environment

PRINTED AND BOUND BY THE MPG BOOKS GROUP LTD, BODMIN, CORNWALL

THANKYOU!

FOR ADVICE, HELP AND SUPPORT...

DAN FRANKLIN AND ALL AT JONATHAN CAPE, SUE PALMER, SIMON ROBERTS,
LUCY ROBERTS, KRISTEN GRAYEWSKI, HOLLY ABNEY, TOM STUBBS, DAVID WILLIAMS,
DR. HANNAH CONDRY, CHARLIE GRAY, JOEL WILSON, ANNA KNOWLES, ANNE HEALEY,
ROB ASH, ALISON CROSS, PAOLO DAVANZO, LISA MARR, BEN O'LEARY & THE HERE SHOP,
PAUL WINTERHART, NICOLE FROBUSCH, SOMERSET LIBRARY SERVICE, PHILL PAYNE,
POSY SIMMONDS, CHRIS STAROS, MY MUM, ALL THE PEOPLE WHO MADE ALL THE
(MOSTLY SAD SOUNDING) MUSIC I CONSTANTLY LISTENED TO WHILE DRAWING,
AND MOST OF ALL TO MY DAD FOR WORDS HELP; AND TO TOM COPS AND NAT BAIRD —
WITHOUT WHOM THIS BOOK WOULDN'T EXIST!

I LOVE POST! IF YOU FEEL LIKE IT, WRITE TO ME C/O:
JONATHAN CAPE,
RANDOM HOUSE,
20 VAUXHALL BRIDGE RD,
LONDON SW1V 2SA

BAGNOLD

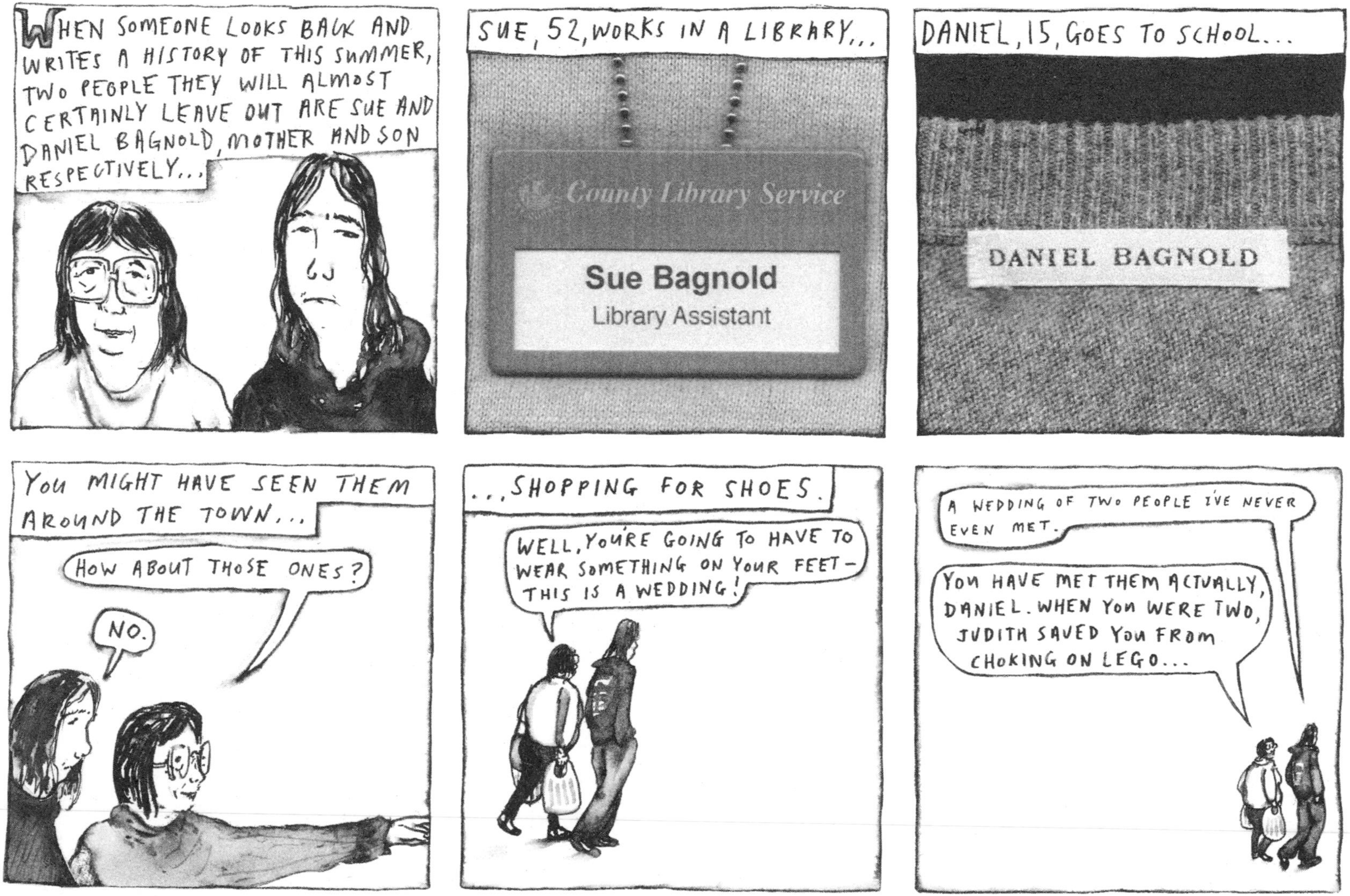
WHEN SOMEONE LOOKS BACK AND WRITES A HISTORY OF THIS SUMMER, TWO PEOPLE THEY WILL ALMOST CERTAINLY LEAVE OUT ARE SUE AND DANIEL BAGNOLD, MOTHER AND SON RESPECTIVELY...
SUE, 52, WORKS IN A LIBRARY...
County Library Service
Sue Bagnold
Library Assistant
DANIEL, 15, GOES TO SCHOOL...
DANIEL BAGNOLD
YOU MIGHT HAVE SEEN THEM AROUND THE TOWN...
HOW ABOUT THOSE ONES?
NO.
...SHOPPING FOR SHOES.
WELL, YOU'RE GOING TO HAVE TO WEAR SOMETHING ON YOUR FEET – THIS IS A WEDDING!
A WEDDING OF TWO PEOPLE I'VE NEVER EVEN MET.
YOU HAVE MET THEM ACTUALLY, DANIEL. WHEN YOU WERE TWO, JUDITH SAVED YOU FROM CHOKING ON LEGO...

FIRST WEEK

SORRY

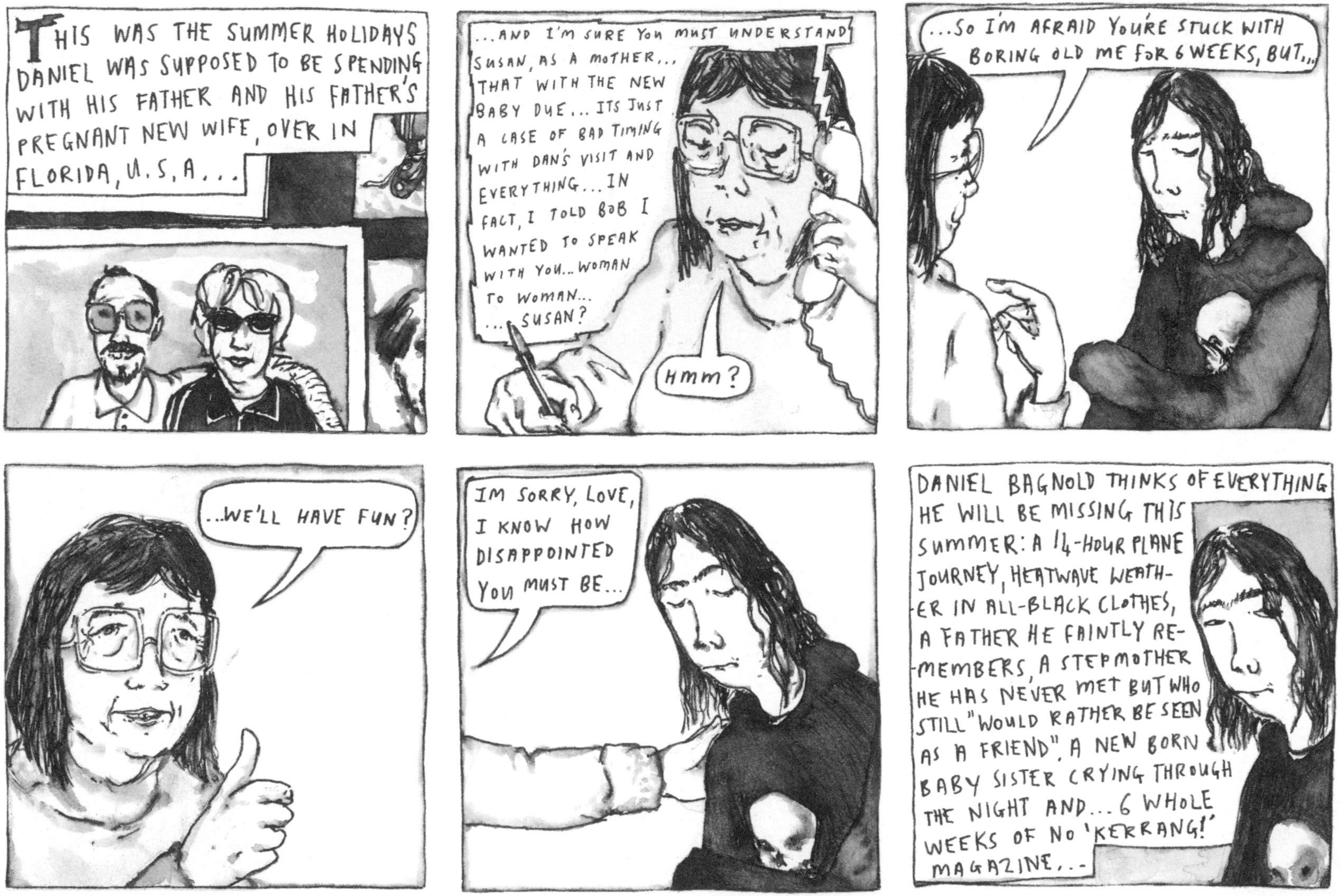
THIS WAS THE SUMMER HOLIDAYS DANIEL WAS SUPPOSED TO BE SPENDING WITH HIS FATHER AND HIS FATHER'S PREGNANT NEW WIFE, OVER IN FLORIDA, U.S.A...
...AND I'M SURE YOU MUST UNDERSTAND SUSAN, AS A MOTHER... THAT WITH THE NEW BABY DUE... ITS JUST A CASE OF BAD TIMING WITH DAN'S VISIT AND EVERYTHING... IN FACT, I TOLD BOB I WANTED TO SPEAK WITH YOU... WOMAN TO WOMAN... ...SUSAN?
HMM?
...SO I'M AFRAID YOU'RE STUCK WITH BORING OLD ME FOR 6 WEEKS, BUT...
...WE'LL HAVE FUN?
IM SORRY, LOVE, I KNOW HOW DISAPPOINTED YOU MUST BE...
DANIEL BAGNOLD THINKS OF EVERYTHING HE WILL BE MISSING THIS SUMMER: A 14-HOUR PLANE JOURNEY, HEATWAVE WEATH-ER IN ALL-BLACK CLOTHES, A FATHER HE FAINTLY RE-MEMBERS, A STEPMOTHER HE HAS NEVER MET BUT WHO STILL "WOULD RATHER BE SEEN AS A FRIEND", A NEW BORN BABY SISTER CRYING THROUGH THE NIGHT AND... 6 WHOLE WEEKS OF NO 'KERRANG!' MAGAZINE...

SKULL

AS SUE WASHES UP...

SHE THINKS OF HOW EVERY MAN IN HER LIFE HAS LEFT HER FOR THE UNITED STATES...

HER FATHER, THE AMERICAN G.I WHO MARRIED HER MOTHER DURING THE WAR, BUT LEFT TO GO BACK TO AMERICA WHEN SUE WAS SEVEN...

...AND HER EX-HUSBAND BOB, WHO WENT AWAY TO FLORIDA "ON BUSINESS" AND NEVER CAME BACK...

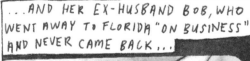

UPSTAIRS, DANIEL IS IN THE BATH. HE IS THINKING OF THE BADGER SKULL HE HAS DRAWN FOR HIS GCSE ART COURSEWORK...

HE IS PARTICULARLY PLEASED WITH THE SHADING...

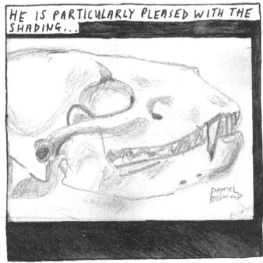

NAMES

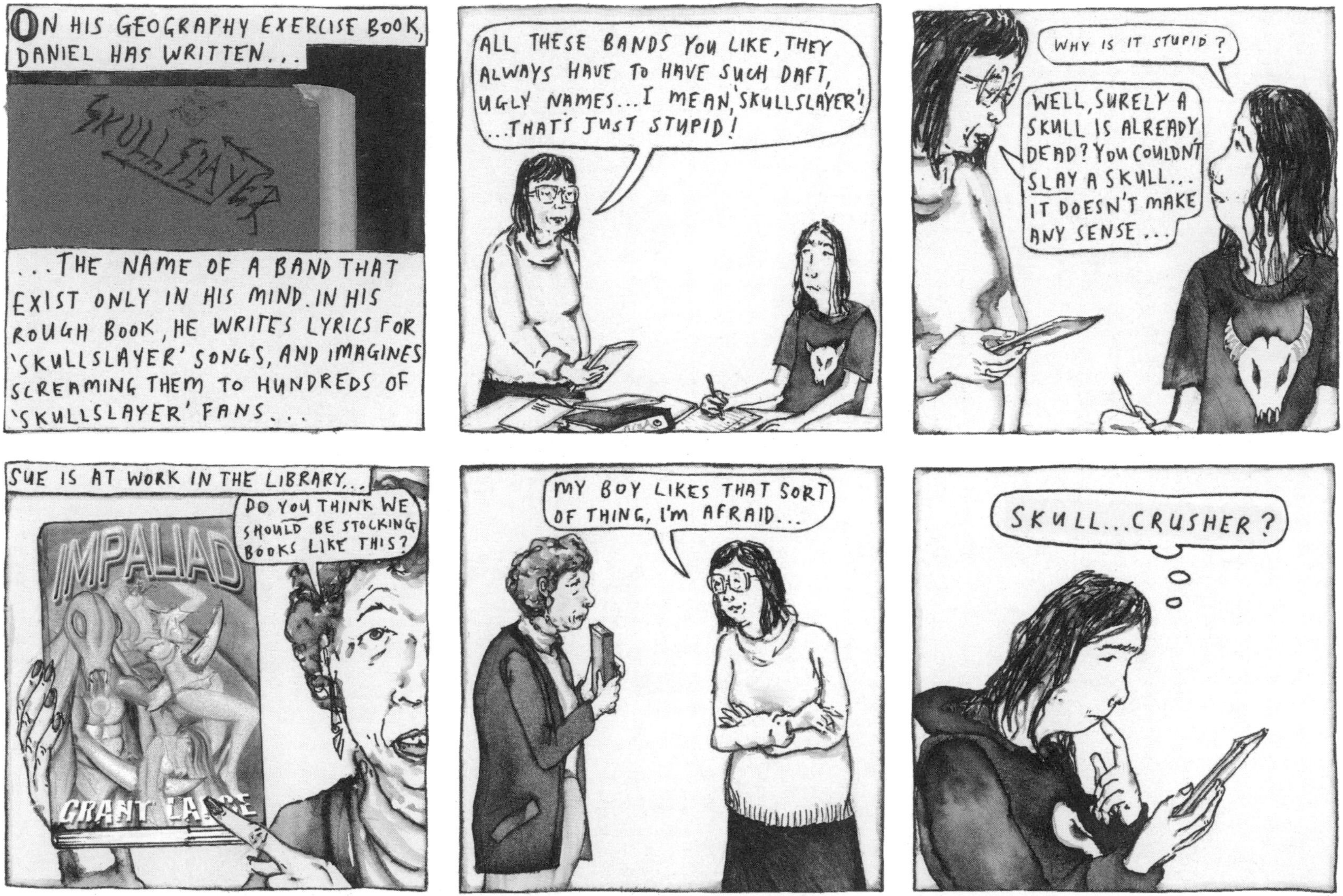
ON HIS GEOGRAPHY EXERCISE BOOK, DANIEL HAS WRITTEN...
SKULLSLAYER
...THE NAME OF A BAND THAT EXIST ONLY IN HIS MIND. IN HIS ROUGH BOOK, HE WRITES LYRICS FOR 'SKULLSLAYER' SONGS, AND IMAGINES SCREAMING THEM TO HUNDREDS OF 'SKULLSLAYER' FANS...
ALL THESE BANDS YOU LIKE, THEY ALWAYS HAVE TO HAVE SUCH DAFT, UGLY NAMES... I MEAN, 'SKULLSLAYER'! ...THAT'S JUST STUPID!
WHY IS IT STUPID?
WELL, SURELY A SKULL IS ALREADY DEAD? YOU COULDN'T SLAY A SKULL... IT DOESN'T MAKE ANY SENSE...
SUE IS AT WORK IN THE LIBRARY...
DO YOU THINK WE SHOULD BE STOCKING BOOKS LIKE THIS?
IMPALIAD
MY BOY LIKES THAT SORT OF THING, I'M AFRAID...
SKULL...CRUSHER?

HAIR

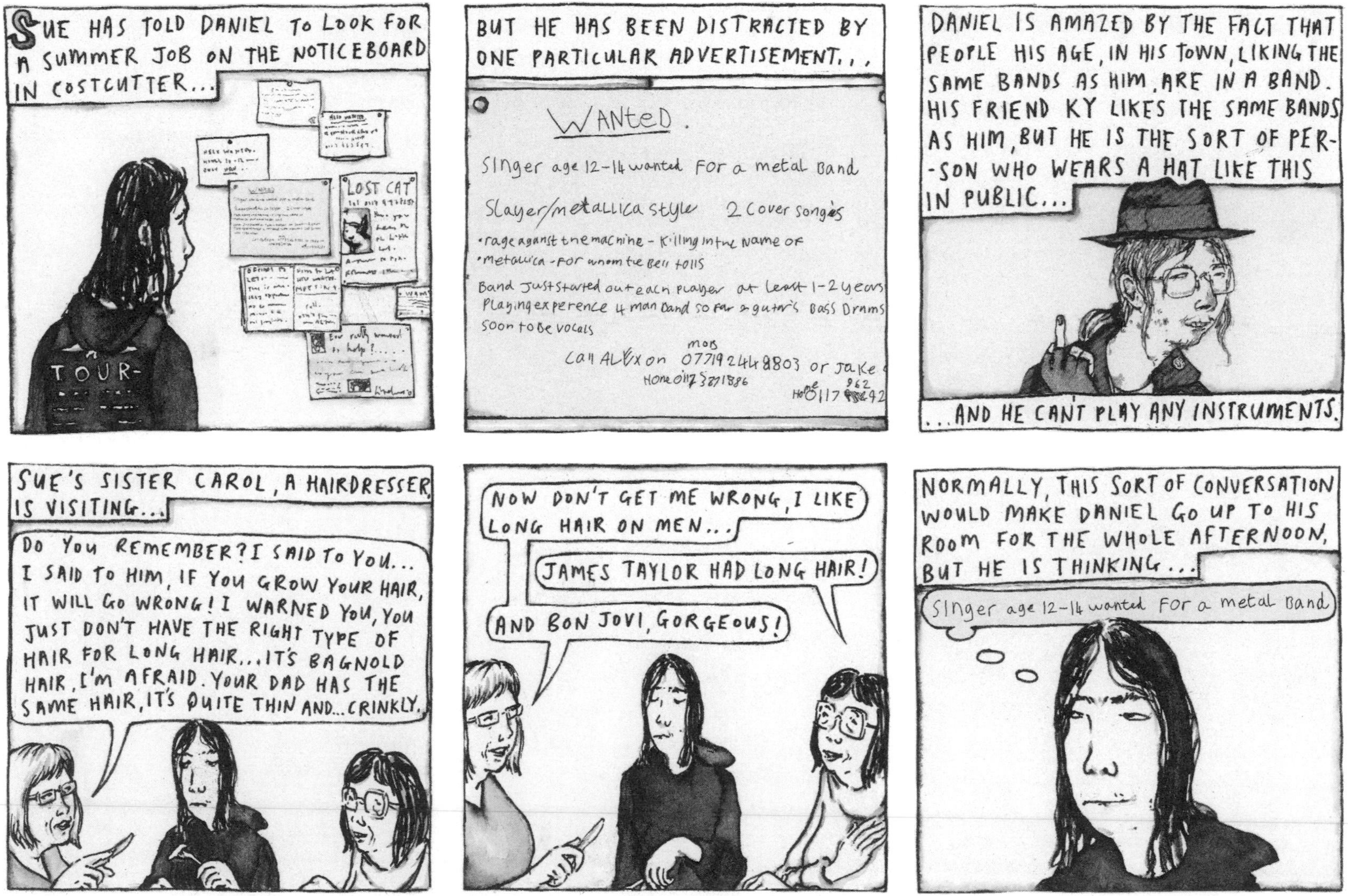

SUE HAS TOLD DANIEL TO LOOK FOR A SUMMER JOB ON THE NOTICEBOARD IN COSTCUTTER...
LOST CAT
TOUR
BUT HE HAS BEEN DISTRACTED BY ONE PARTICULAR ADVERTISEMENT...
WANTED.
Singer age 12-14 wanted For a metal Band
Slayer/metallica style 2 cover songs
•rage against the machine - Killing in the name of
•metallica - For whom the Bell tolls
Band Just started out each player at least 1-2 years Playing experence 4 man band so far 2 guitar's Bass Drams soon to Be vocals
Call ALEX on mob 07719244803 or Jake
DANIEL IS AMAZED BY THE FACT THAT PEOPLE HIS AGE, IN HIS TOWN, LIKING THE SAME BANDS AS HIM, ARE IN A BAND. HIS FRIEND KY LIKES THE SAME BANDS AS HIM, BUT HE IS THE SORT OF PERSON WHO WEARS A HAT LIKE THIS IN PUBLIC...
...AND HE CAN'T PLAY ANY INSTRUMENTS.
SUE'S SISTER CAROL, A HAIRDRESSER, IS VISITING...
DO YOU REMEMBER? I SAID TO YOU... I SAID TO HIM, IF YOU GROW YOUR HAIR, IT WILL GO WRONG! I WARNED YOU, YOU JUST DON'T HAVE THE RIGHT TYPE OF HAIR FOR LONG HAIR... IT'S BAGNOLD HAIR, I'M AFRAID. YOUR DAD HAS THE SAME HAIR, IT'S QUITE THIN AND... CRINKLY.
NOW DON'T GET ME WRONG, I LIKE LONG HAIR ON MEN...
JAMES TAYLOR HAD LONG HAIR!
AND BON JOVI, GORGEOUS!
NORMALLY, THIS SORT OF CONVERSATION WOULD MAKE DANIEL GO UP TO HIS ROOM FOR THE WHOLE AFTERNOON, BUT HE IS THINKING...
Singer age 12-14 wanted For a metal Band

RECORDS

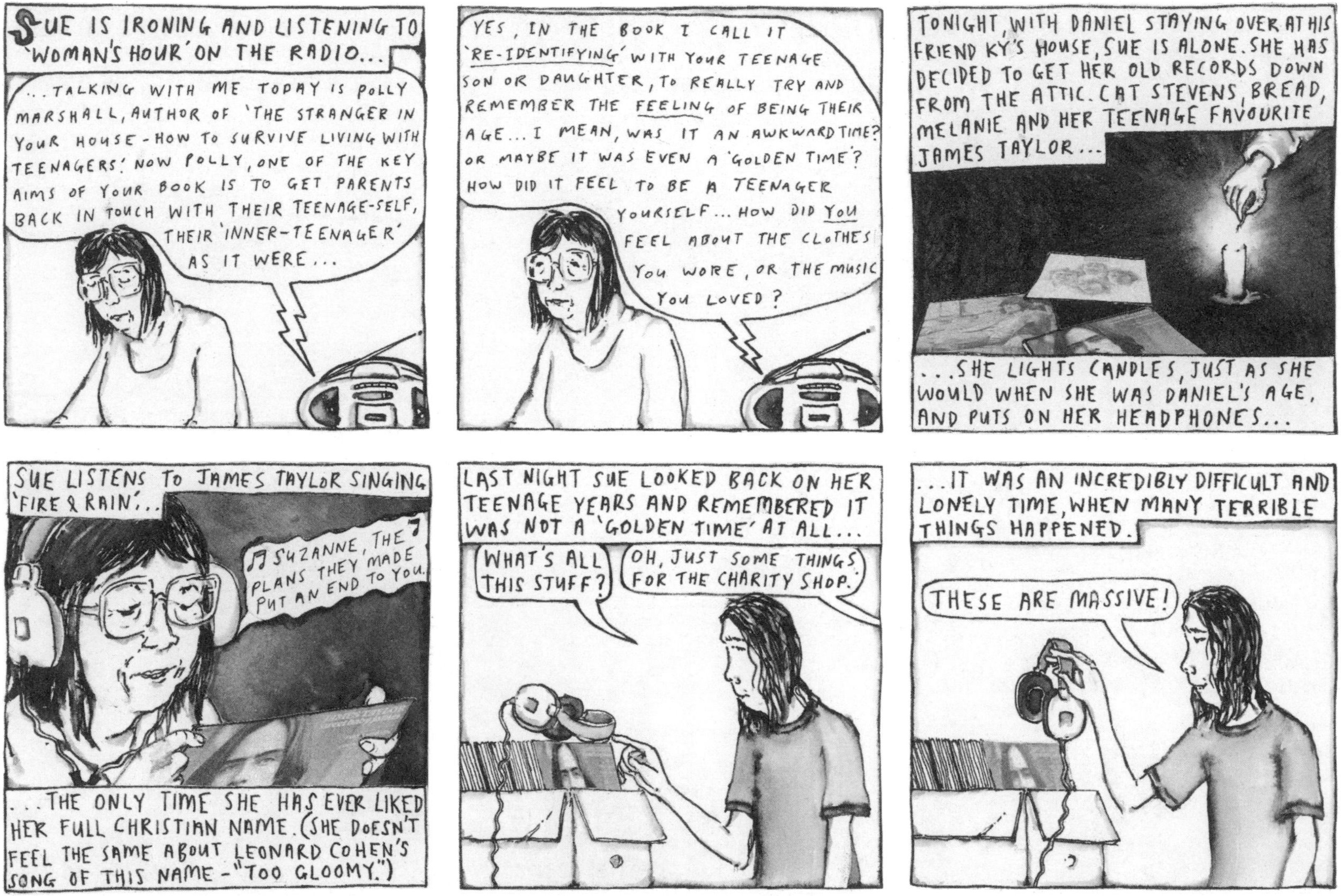
SUE IS IRONING AND LISTENING TO 'WOMAN'S HOUR' ON THE RADIO...
...TALKING WITH ME TODAY IS POLLY MARSHALL, AUTHOR OF 'THE STRANGER IN YOUR HOUSE - HOW TO SURVIVE LIVING WITH TEENAGERS.' NOW POLLY, ONE OF THE KEY AIMS OF YOUR BOOK IS TO GET PARENTS BACK IN TOUCH WITH THEIR TEENAGE-SELF, THEIR 'INNER-TEENAGER' AS IT WERE...
YES, IN THE BOOK I CALL IT 'RE-IDENTIFYING' WITH YOUR TEENAGE SON OR DAUGHTER, TO REALLY TRY AND REMEMBER THE FEELING OF BEING THEIR AGE... I MEAN, WAS IT AN AWKWARD TIME? OR MAYBE IT WAS EVEN A 'GOLDEN TIME'? HOW DID IT FEEL TO BE A TEENAGER YOURSELF... HOW DID YOU FEEL ABOUT THE CLOTHES YOU WORE, OR THE MUSIC YOU LOVED?
TONIGHT, WITH DANIEL STAYING OVER AT HIS FRIEND KY'S HOUSE, SUE IS ALONE. SHE HAS DECIDED TO GET HER OLD RECORDS DOWN FROM THE ATTIC. CAT STEVENS, BREAD, MELANIE AND HER TEENAGE FAVOURITE JAMES TAYLOR...
...SHE LIGHTS CANDLES, JUST AS SHE WOULD WHEN SHE WAS DANIEL'S AGE, AND PUTS ON HER HEADPHONES...
SUE LISTENS TO JAMES TAYLOR SINGING 'FIRE & RAIN'...
♫ SUZANNE, THE PLANS THEY MADE PUT AN END TO YOU. ♪
...THE ONLY TIME SHE HAS EVER LIKED HER FULL CHRISTIAN NAME. (SHE DOESN'T FEEL THE SAME ABOUT LEONARD COHEN'S SONG OF THIS NAME - "TOO GLOOMY.")
LAST NIGHT SUE LOOKED BACK ON HER TEENAGE YEARS AND REMEMBERED IT WAS NOT A 'GOLDEN TIME' AT ALL...
WHAT'S ALL THIS STUFF?
OH, JUST SOME THINGS FOR THE CHARITY SHOP.
...IT WAS AN INCREDIBLY DIFFICULT AND LONELY TIME, WHEN MANY TERRIBLE THINGS HAPPENED.
THESE ARE MASSIVE!

SELF-EXPRESSION

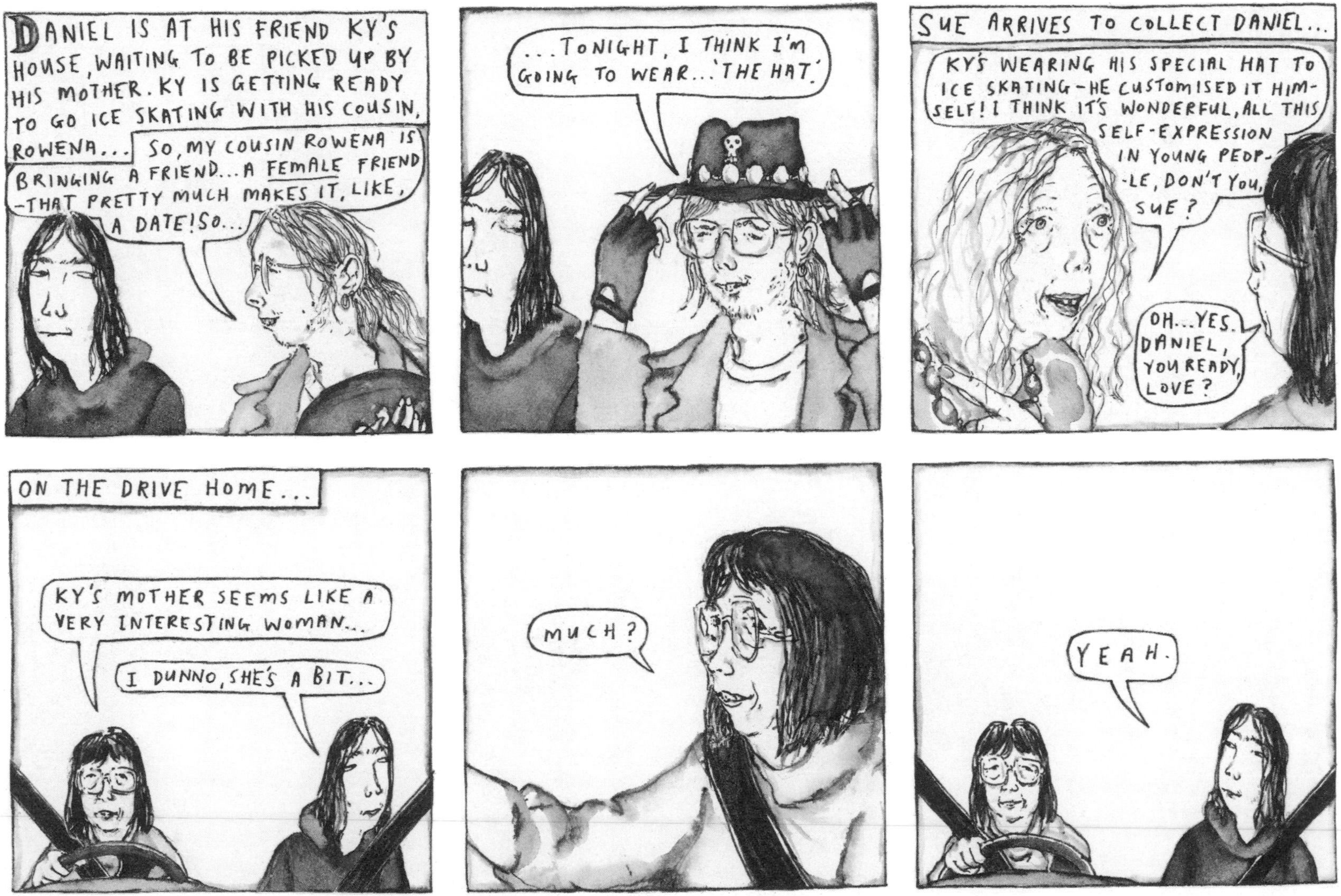
DANIEL IS AT HIS FRIEND KY'S HOUSE, WAITING TO BE PICKED UP BY HIS MOTHER. KY IS GETTING READY TO GO ICE SKATING WITH HIS COUSIN, ROWENA...
SO, MY COUSIN ROWENA IS BRINGING A FRIEND... A FEMALE FRIEND -THAT PRETTY MUCH MAKES IT, LIKE, A DATE! SO...
...TONIGHT, I THINK I'M GOING TO WEAR... 'THE HAT.'
SUE ARRIVES TO COLLECT DANIEL...
KY'S WEARING HIS SPECIAL HAT TO ICE SKATING - HE CUSTOMISED IT HIMSELF! I THINK IT'S WONDERFUL, ALL THIS SELF-EXPRESSION IN YOUNG PEOPLE, DON'T YOU, SUE?
OH... YES. DANIEL, YOU READY, LOVE?
ON THE DRIVE HOME...
KY'S MOTHER SEEMS LIKE A VERY INTERESTING WOMAN...
I DUNNO, SHE'S A BIT...
MUCH?
YEAH.

NUMBER

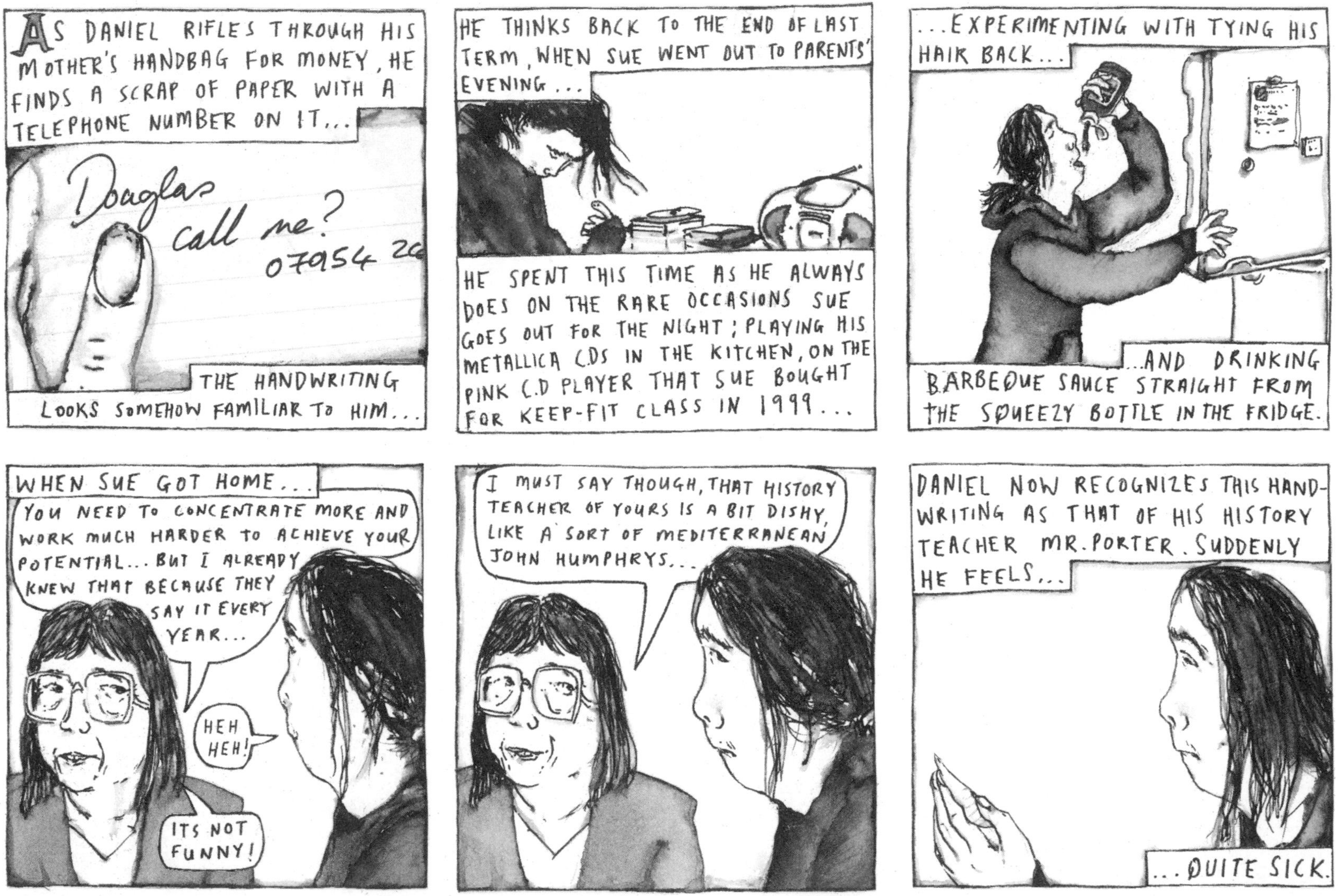

AS DANIEL RIFLES THROUGH HIS MOTHER'S HANDBAG FOR MONEY, HE FINDS A SCRAP OF PAPER WITH A TELEPHONE NUMBER ON IT...
Douglas call me?
07954 2
THE HANDWRITING LOOKS SOMEHOW FAMILIAR TO HIM...
HE THINKS BACK TO THE END OF LAST TERM, WHEN SUE WENT OUT TO PARENTS' EVENING...
HE SPENT THIS TIME AS HE ALWAYS DOES ON THE RARE OCCASIONS SUE GOES OUT FOR THE NIGHT; PLAYING HIS METALLICA C.DS IN THE KITCHEN, ON THE PINK C.D PLAYER THAT SUE BOUGHT FOR KEEP-FIT CLASS IN 1999...
...EXPERIMENTING WITH TYING HIS HAIR BACK...
...AND DRINKING BARBEQUE SAUCE STRAIGHT FROM THE SQUEEZY BOTTLE IN THE FRIDGE.
WHEN SUE GOT HOME...
YOU NEED TO CONCENTRATE MORE AND WORK MUCH HARDER TO ACHIEVE YOUR POTENTIAL... BUT I ALREADY KNEW THAT BECAUSE THEY SAY IT EVERY YEAR...
HEH HEH!
ITS NOT FUNNY!
I MUST SAY THOUGH, THAT HISTORY TEACHER OF YOURS IS A BIT DISHY, LIKE A SORT OF MEDITERRANEAN JOHN HUMPHRYS...
DANIEL NOW RECOGNIZES THIS HAND-WRITING AS THAT OF HIS HISTORY TEACHER MR. PORTER. SUDDENLY HE FEELS...
...QUITE SICK.

DOG

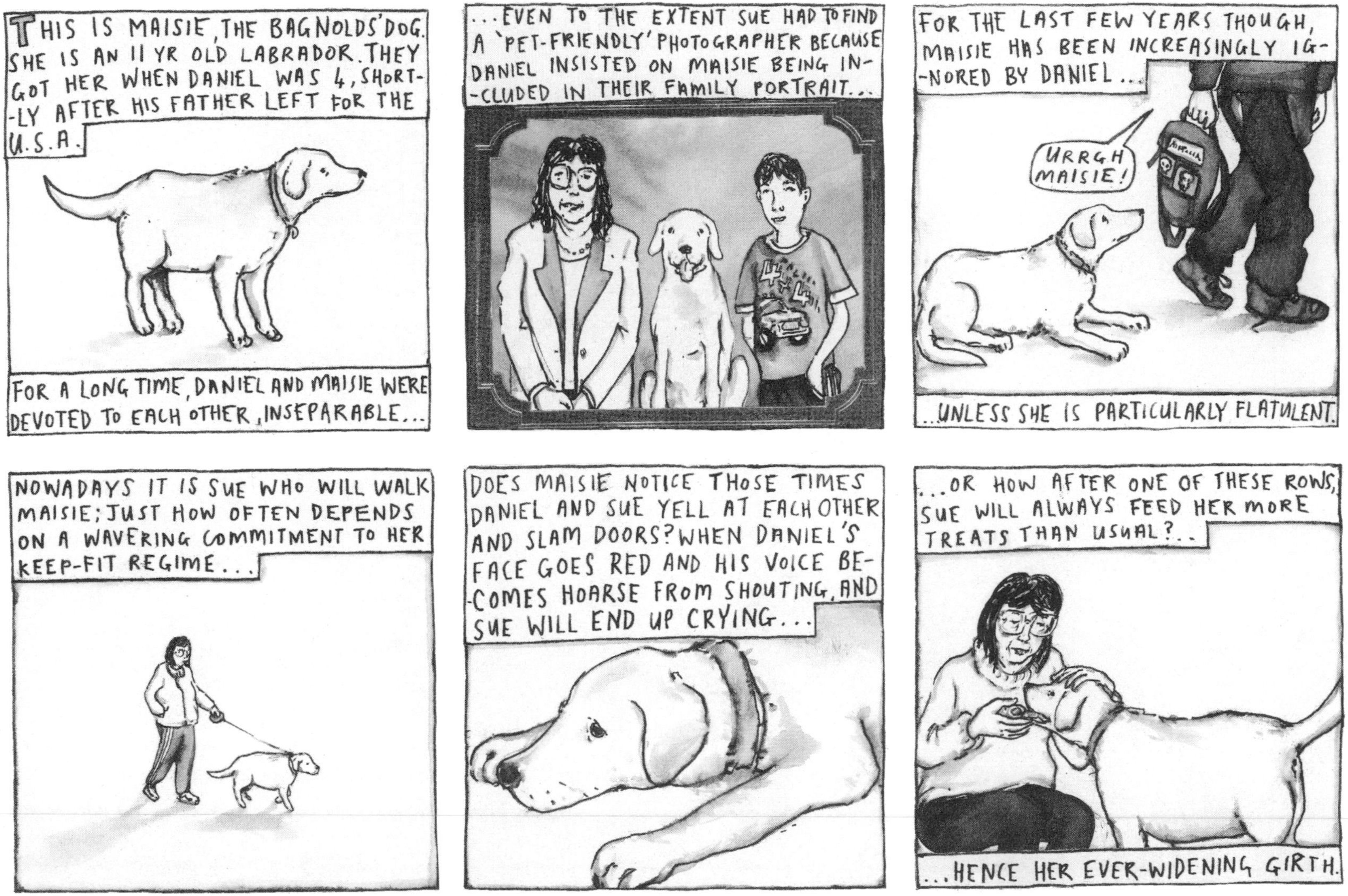
THIS IS MAISIE, THE BAGNOLDS' DOG. SHE IS AN 11 YR OLD LABRADOR. THEY GOT HER WHEN DANIEL WAS 4, SHORT- -LY AFTER HIS FATHER LEFT FOR THE U.S.A.
FOR A LONG TIME, DANIEL AND MAISIE WERE DEVOTED TO EACH OTHER, INSEPARABLE...
...EVEN TO THE EXTENT SUE HAD TO FIND A 'PET-FRIENDLY' PHOTOGRAPHER BECAUSE DANIEL INSISTED ON MAISIE BEING IN- -CLUDED IN THEIR FAMILY PORTRAIT...
FOR THE LAST FEW YEARS THOUGH, MAISIE HAS BEEN INCREASINGLY IG- -NORED BY DANIEL...
URRGH MAISIE!
...UNLESS SHE IS PARTICULARLY FLATULENT.
NOWADAYS IT IS SUE WHO WILL WALK MAISIE; JUST HOW OFTEN DEPENDS ON A WAVERING COMMITMENT TO HER KEEP-FIT REGIME...
DOES MAISIE NOTICE THOSE TIMES DANIEL AND SUE YELL AT EACH OTHER AND SLAM DOORS? WHEN DANIEL'S FACE GOES RED AND HIS VOICE BE- -COMES HOARSE FROM SHOUTING, AND SUE WILL END UP CRYING...
...OR HOW AFTER ONE OF THESE ROWS, SUE WILL ALWAYS FEED HER MORE TREATS THAN USUAL?...
...HENCE HER EVER-WIDENING GIRTH.

REALISE

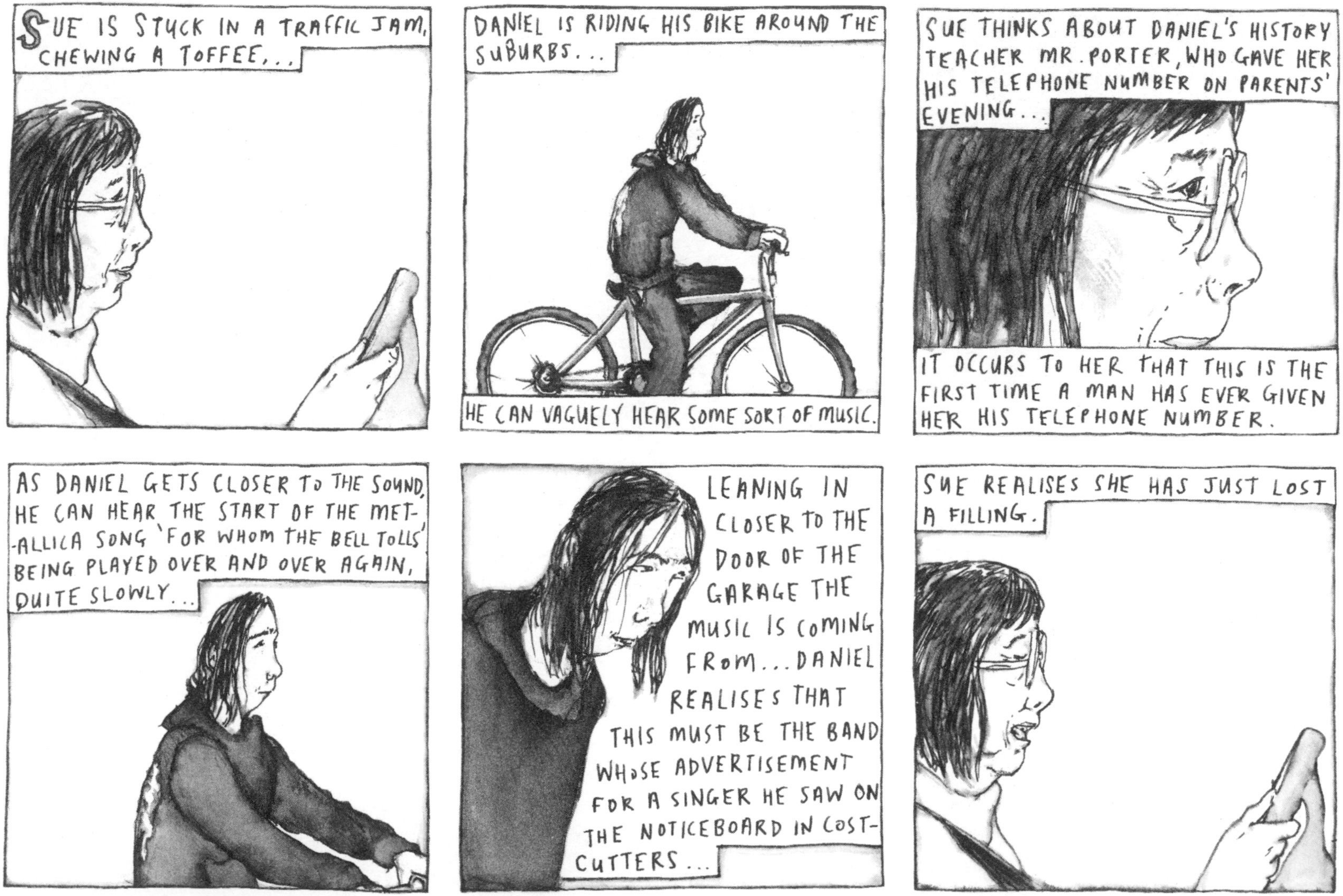
SUE IS STUCK IN A TRAFFIC JAM, CHEWING A TOFFEE...
DANIEL IS RIDING HIS BIKE AROUND THE SUBURBS...
HE CAN VAGUELY HEAR SOME SORT OF MUSIC.
SUE THINKS ABOUT DANIEL'S HISTORY TEACHER MR. PORTER, WHO GAVE HER HIS TELEPHONE NUMBER ON PARENTS' EVENING...
IT OCCURS TO HER THAT THIS IS THE FIRST TIME A MAN HAS EVER GIVEN HER HIS TELEPHONE NUMBER.
AS DANIEL GETS CLOSER TO THE SOUND, HE CAN HEAR THE START OF THE MET-ALLICA SONG 'FOR WHOM THE BELL TOLLS' BEING PLAYED OVER AND OVER AGAIN, QUITE SLOWLY...
LEANING IN CLOSER TO THE DOOR OF THE GARAGE THE MUSIC IS COMING FROM... DANIEL REALISES THAT THIS MUST BE THE BAND WHOSE ADVERTISEMENT FOR A SINGER HE SAW ON THE NOTICEBOARD IN COST-CUTTERS...
SUE REALISES SHE HAS JUST LOST A FILLING.

TOUR

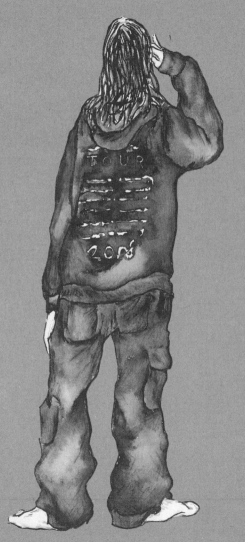

SECOND WEEK

OPPOSITE

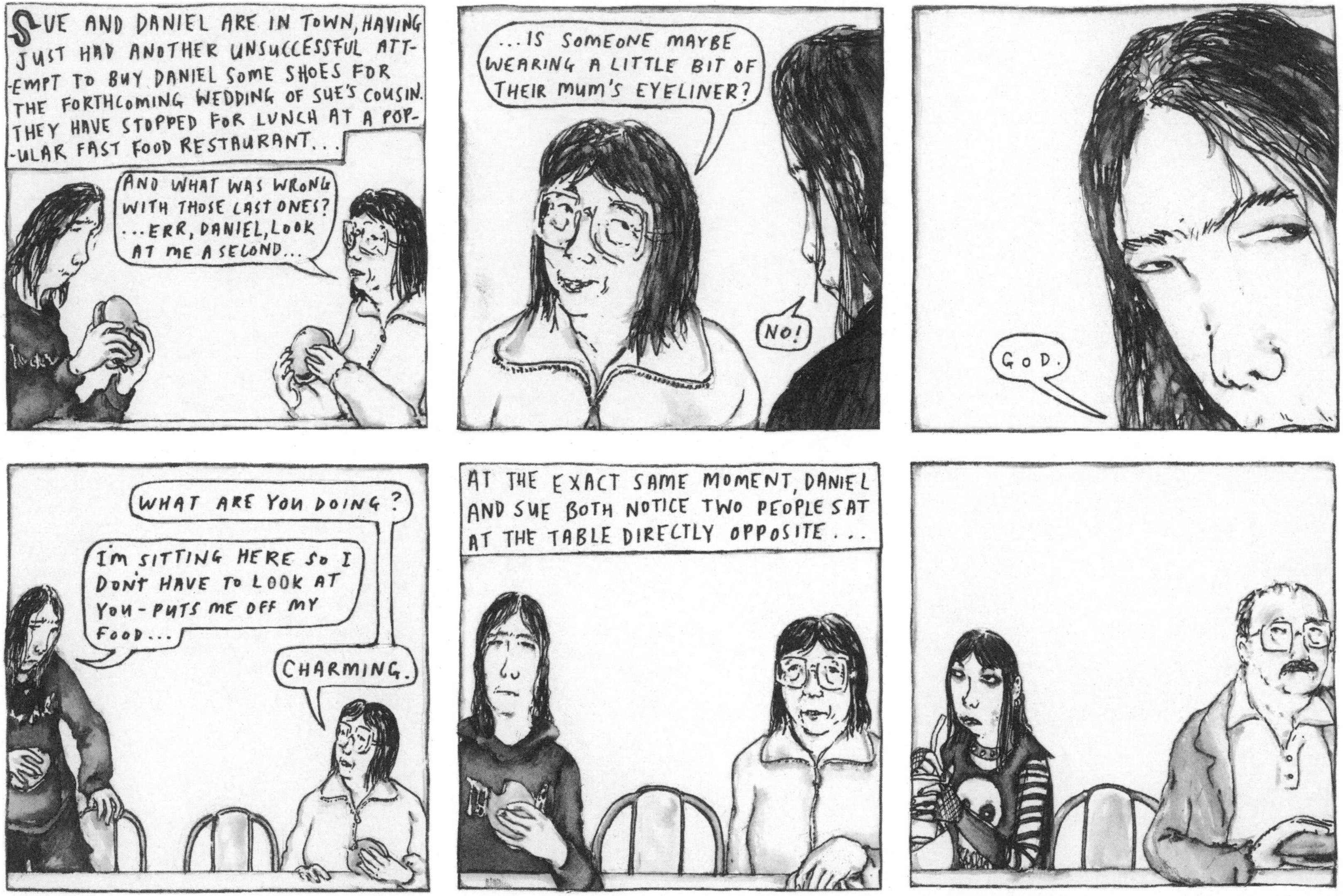
SUE AND DANIEL ARE IN TOWN, HAVING JUST HAD ANOTHER UNSUCCESSFUL ATT-EMPT TO BUY DANIEL SOME SHOES FOR THE FORTHCOMING WEDDING OF SUE'S COUSIN. THEY HAVE STOPPED FOR LUNCH AT A POP-ULAR FAST FOOD RESTAURANT...
AND WHAT WAS WRONG WITH THOSE LAST ONES? ...ERR, DANIEL, LOOK AT ME A SECOND...
...IS SOMEONE MAYBE WEARING A LITTLE BIT OF THEIR MUM'S EYELINER?
NO!
GOD.
WHAT ARE YOU DOING?
I'M SITTING HERE SO I DON'T HAVE TO LOOK AT YOU - PUTS ME OFF MY FOOD...
CHARMING.
AT THE EXACT SAME MOMENT, DANIEL AND SUE BOTH NOTICE TWO PEOPLE SAT AT THE TABLE DIRECTLY OPPOSITE...

SOLO

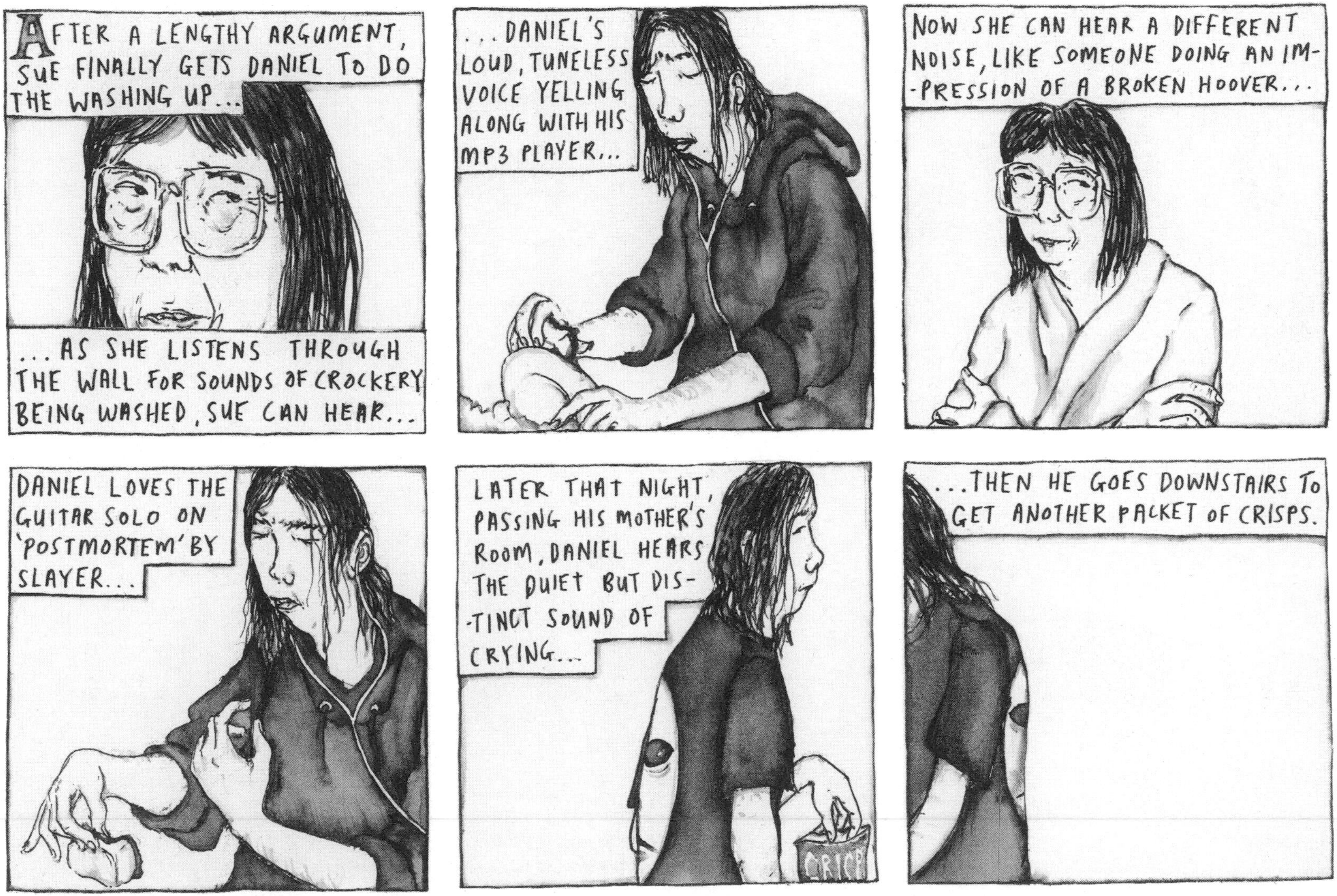
AFTER A LENGTHY ARGUMENT, SUE FINALLY GETS DANIEL TO DO THE WASHING UP...
...AS SHE LISTENS THROUGH THE WALL FOR SOUNDS OF CROCKERY BEING WASHED, SUE CAN HEAR...
...DANIEL'S LOUD, TUNELESS VOICE YELLING ALONG WITH HIS MP3 PLAYER...
NOW SHE CAN HEAR A DIFFERENT NOISE, LIKE SOMEONE DOING AN IM-PRESSION OF A BROKEN HOOVER...
DANIEL LOVES THE GUITAR SOLO ON 'POSTMORTEM' BY SLAYER...
LATER THAT NIGHT, PASSING HIS MOTHER'S ROOM, DANIEL HEARS THE QUIET BUT DIS-TINCT SOUND OF CRYING...
...THEN HE GOES DOWNSTAIRS TO GET ANOTHER PACKET OF CRISPS.

HABIT

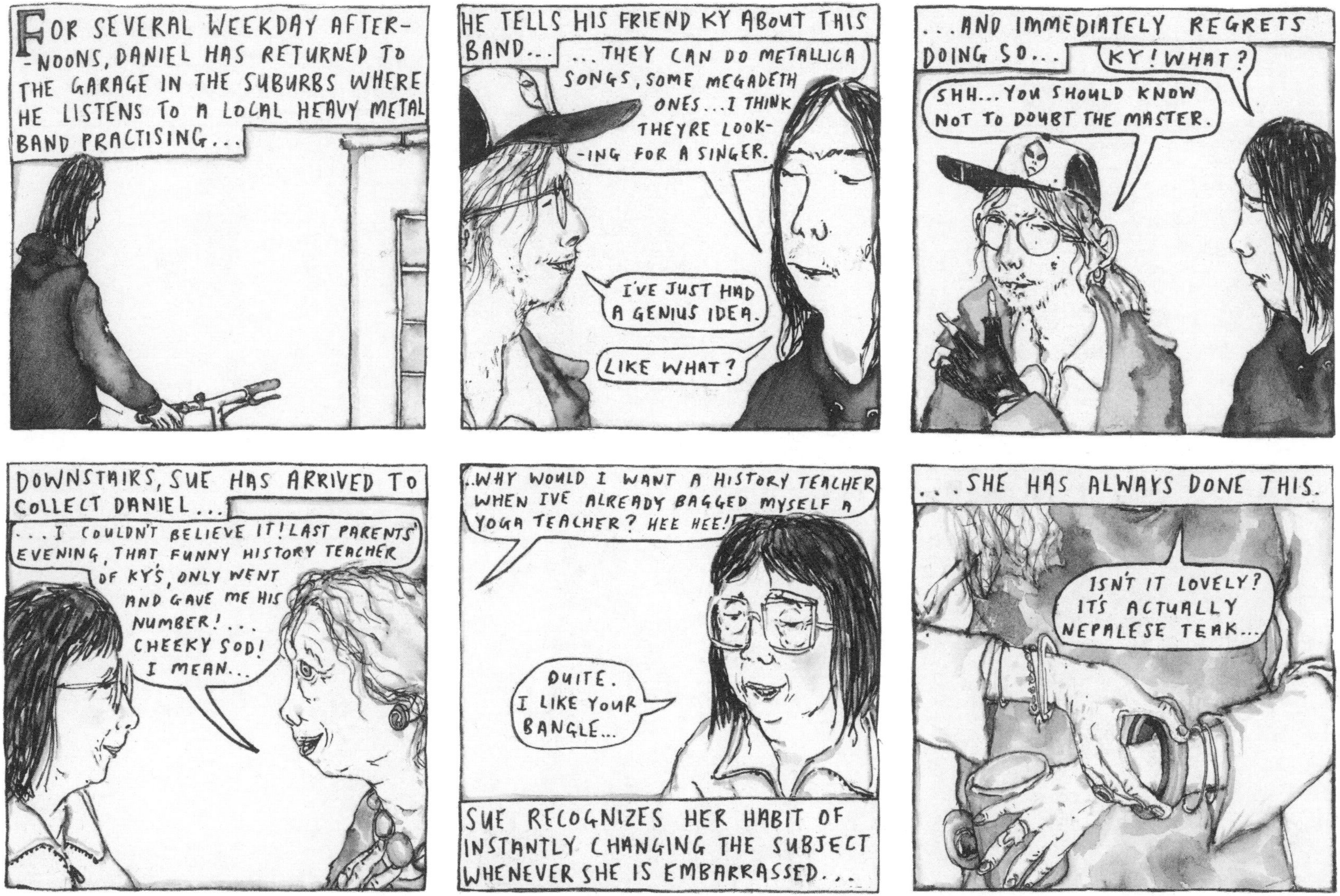
FOR SEVERAL WEEKDAY AFTER-NOONS, DANIEL HAS RETURNED TO THE GARAGE IN THE SUBURBS WHERE HE LISTENS TO A LOCAL HEAVY METAL BAND PRACTISING...
HE TELLS HIS FRIEND KY ABOUT THIS BAND...
...THEY CAN DO METALLICA SONGS, SOME MEGADETH ONES... I THINK THEYRE LOOK-ING FOR A SINGER.
I'VE JUST HAD A GENIUS IDEA.
LIKE WHAT?
...AND IMMEDIATELY REGRETS DOING SO...
KY! WHAT?
SHH... YOU SHOULD KNOW NOT TO DOUBT THE MASTER.
DOWNSTAIRS, SUE HAS ARRIVED TO COLLECT DANIEL...
...I COULDN'T BELIEVE IT! LAST PARENTS' EVENING, THAT FUNNY HISTORY TEACHER OF KY'S, ONLY WENT AND GAVE ME HIS NUMBER!... CHEEKY SOD! I MEAN...
..WHY WOULD I WANT A HISTORY TEACHER WHEN IVE ALREADY BAGGED MYSELF A YOGA TEACHER? HEE HEE!
QUITE. I LIKE YOUR BANGLE...
SUE RECOGNIZES HER HABIT OF INSTANTLY CHANGING THE SUBJECT WHENEVER SHE IS EMBARRASSED...
...SHE HAS ALWAYS DONE THIS.
ISN'T IT LOVELY? IT'S ACTUALLY NEPALESE TEAK...

HOUSE

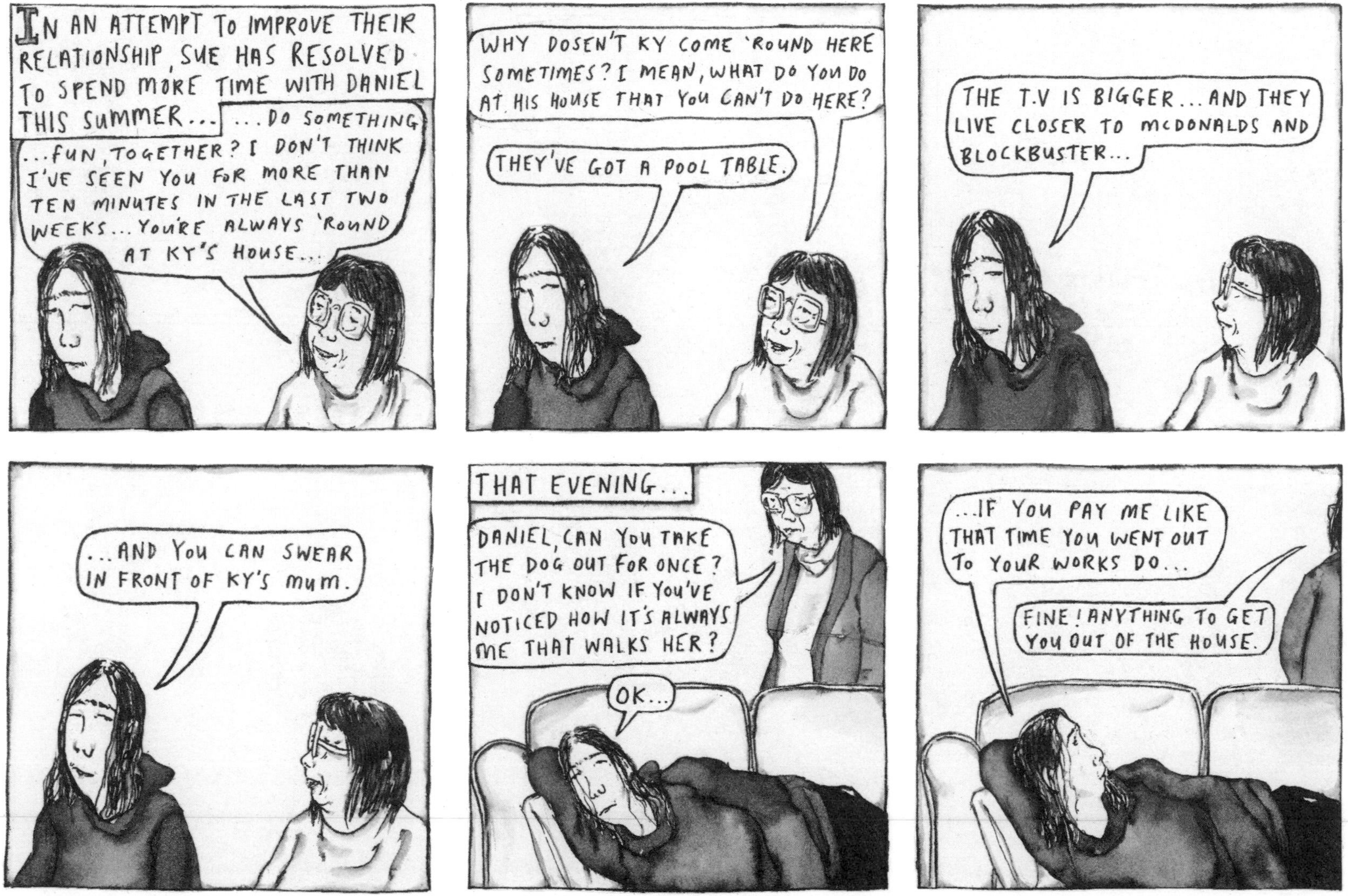
IN AN ATTEMPT TO IMPROVE THEIR RELATIONSHIP, SUE HAS RESOLVED TO SPEND MORE TIME WITH DANIEL THIS SUMMER...
...DO SOMETHING ...FUN, TOGETHER? I DON'T THINK I'VE SEEN YOU FOR MORE THAN TEN MINUTES IN THE LAST TWO WEEKS... YOU'RE ALWAYS 'ROUND AT KY'S HOUSE...
WHY DOSEN'T KY COME 'ROUND HERE SOMETIMES? I MEAN, WHAT DO YOU DO AT HIS HOUSE THAT YOU CAN'T DO HERE?
THEY'VE GOT A POOL TABLE.
THE T.V IS BIGGER... AND THEY LIVE CLOSER TO MCDONALDS AND BLOCKBUSTER...
...AND YOU CAN SWEAR IN FRONT OF KY'S MUM.
THAT EVENING...
DANIEL, CAN YOU TAKE THE DOG OUT FOR ONCE? I DON'T KNOW IF YOU'VE NOTICED HOW IT'S ALWAYS ME THAT WALKS HER?
OK...
...IF YOU PAY ME LIKE THAT TIME YOU WENT OUT TO YOUR WORKS DO...
FINE! ANYTHING TO GET YOU OUT OF THE HOUSE.

BOYS

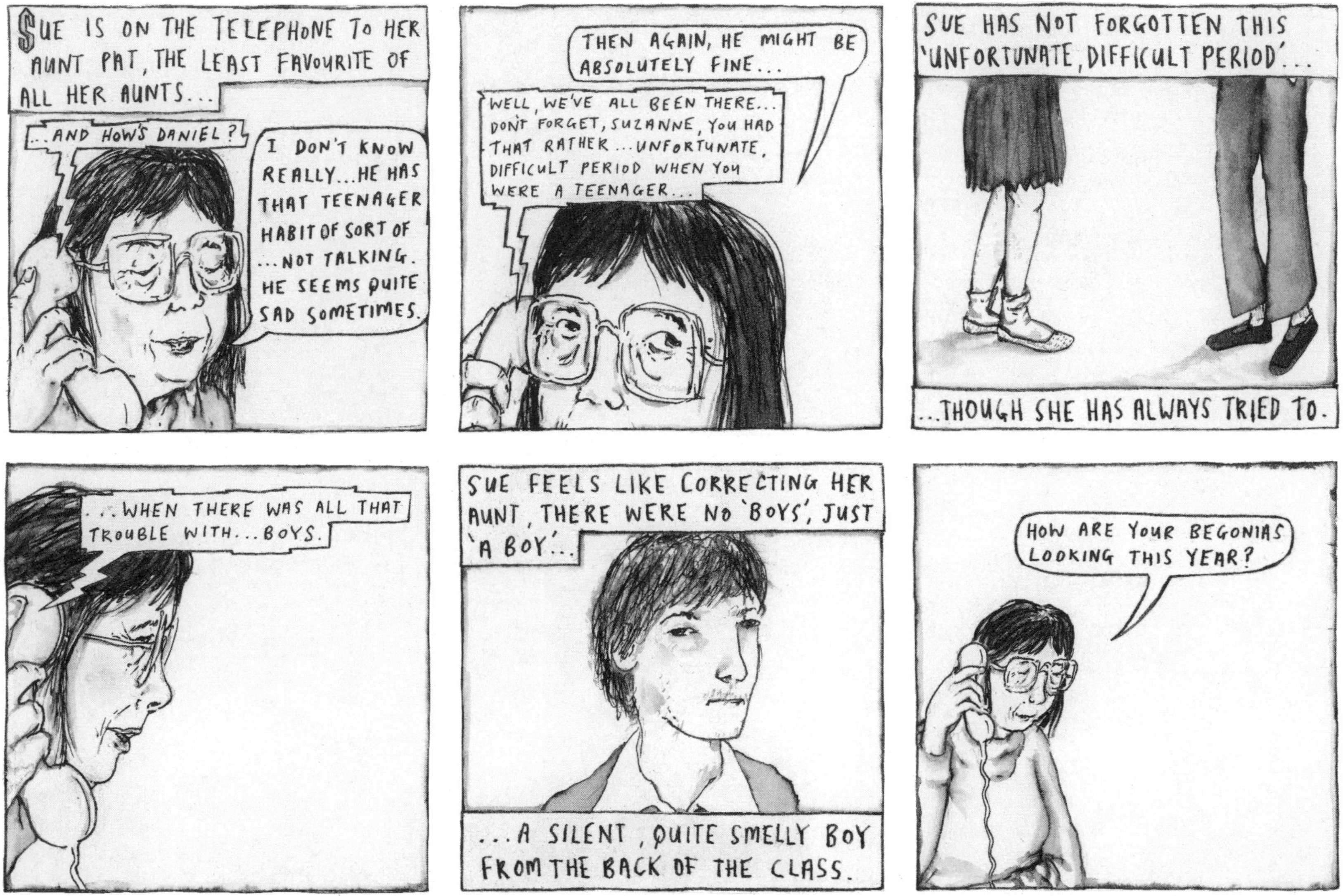
SUE IS ON THE TELEPHONE TO HER AUNT PAT, THE LEAST FAVOURITE OF ALL HER AUNTS...
...AND HOW'S DANIEL?
I DON'T KNOW REALLY... HE HAS THAT TEENAGER HABIT OF SORT OF ...NOT TALKING. HE SEEMS QUITE SAD SOMETIMES.
THEN AGAIN, HE MIGHT BE ABSOLUTELY FINE...
WELL, WE'VE ALL BEEN THERE... DON'T FORGET, SUZANNE, YOU HAD THAT RATHER ...UNFORTUNATE, DIFFICULT PERIOD WHEN YOU WERE A TEENAGER...
SUE HAS NOT FORGOTTEN THIS 'UNFORTUNATE, DIFFICULT PERIOD'...
...THOUGH SHE HAS ALWAYS TRIED TO.
...WHEN THERE WAS ALL THAT TROUBLE WITH...BOYS.
SUE FEELS LIKE CORRECTING HER AUNT, THERE WERE NO 'BOYS', JUST 'A BOY'...
...A SILENT, QUITE SMELLY BOY FROM THE BACK OF THE CLASS.
HOW ARE YOUR BEGONIAS LOOKING THIS YEAR?

TWELVE

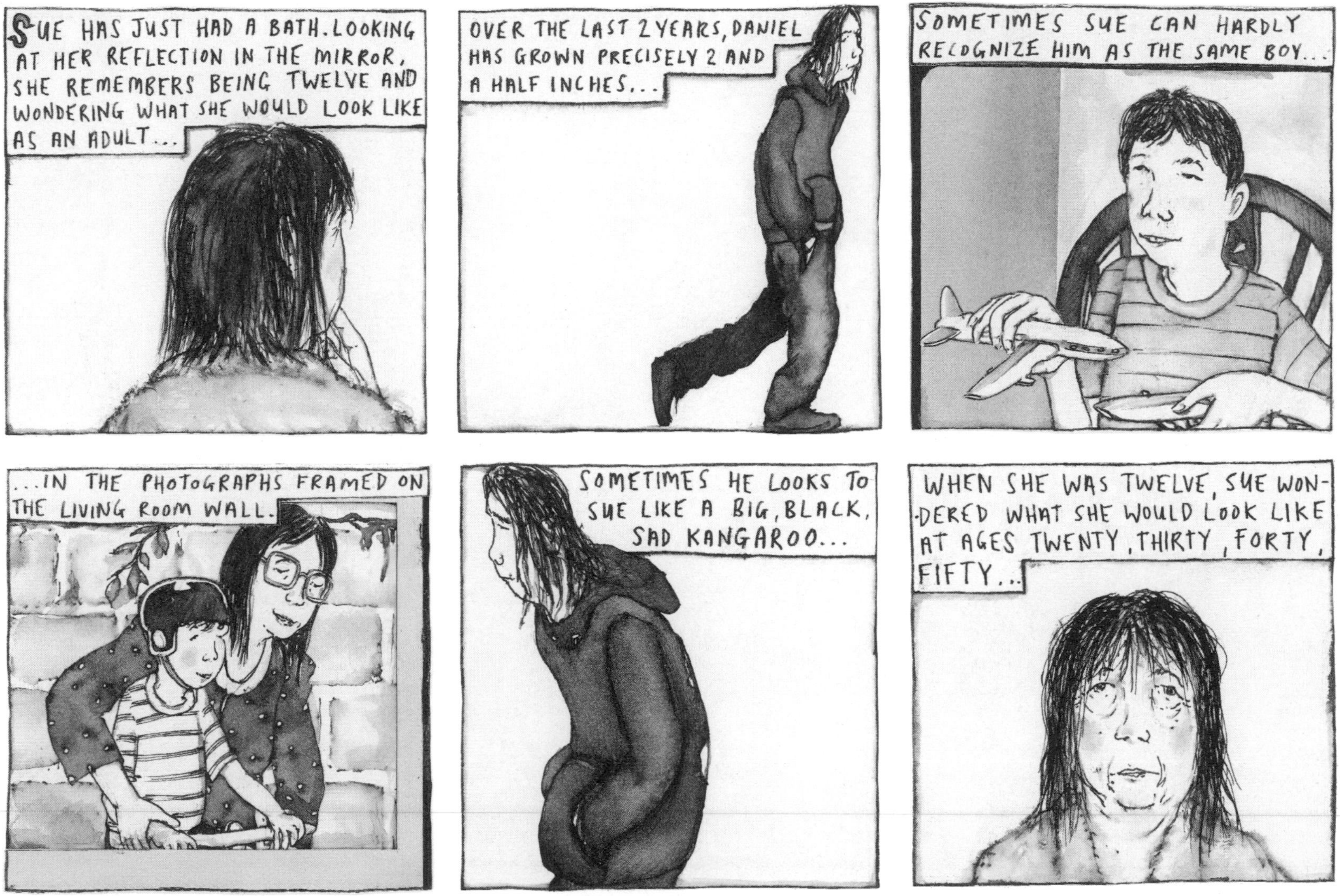
SUE HAS JUST HAD A BATH. LOOKING AT HER REFLECTION IN THE MIRROR, SHE REMEMBERS BEING TWELVE AND WONDERING WHAT SHE WOULD LOOK LIKE AS AN ADULT...
OVER THE LAST 2 YEARS, DANIEL HAS GROWN PRECISELY 2 AND A HALF INCHES...
SOMETIMES SUE CAN HARDLY RECOGNIZE HIM AS THE SAME BOY...
...IN THE PHOTOGRAPHS FRAMED ON THE LIVING ROOM WALL.
SOMETIMES HE LOOKS TO SUE LIKE A BIG, BLACK, SAD KANGAROO...
WHEN SHE WAS TWELVE, SUE WONDERED WHAT SHE WOULD LOOK LIKE AT AGES TWENTY, THIRTY, FORTY, FIFTY...

BIRTHDAY

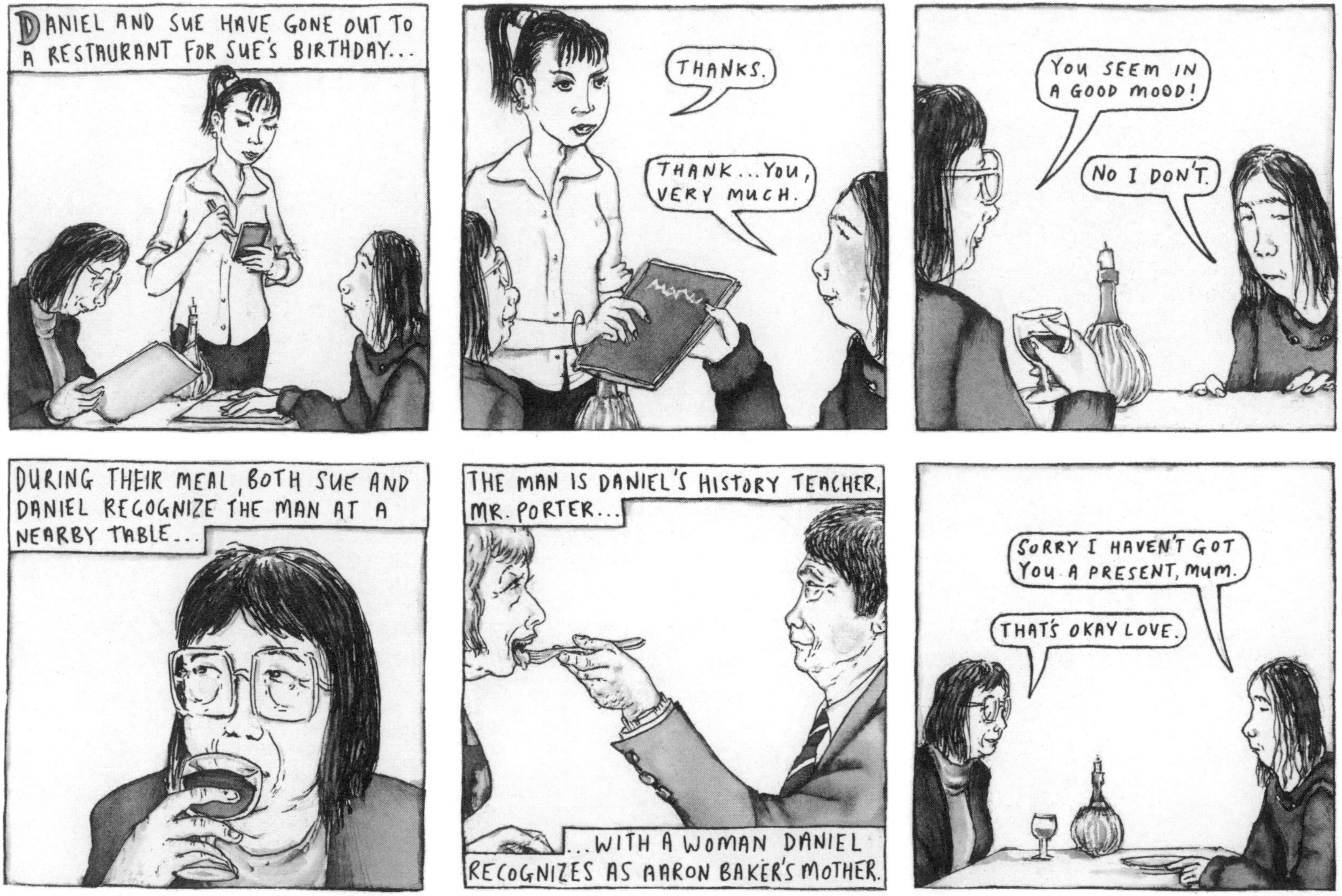
DANIEL AND SUE HAVE GONE OUT TO A RESTAURANT FOR SUE'S BIRTHDAY...
THANKS.
THANK...YOU, VERY MUCH.
YOU SEEM IN A GOOD MOOD!
NO I DON'T.
DURING THEIR MEAL, BOTH SUE AND DANIEL REGOGNIZE THE MAN AT A NEARBY TABLE...
THE MAN IS DANIEL'S HISTORY TEACHER, MR. PORTER...
...WITH A WOMAN DANIEL RECOGNIZES AS AARON BAKER'S MOTHER.
SORRY I HAVEN'T GOT YOU A PRESENT, MUM.
THAT'S OKAY LOVE.

LYRICS

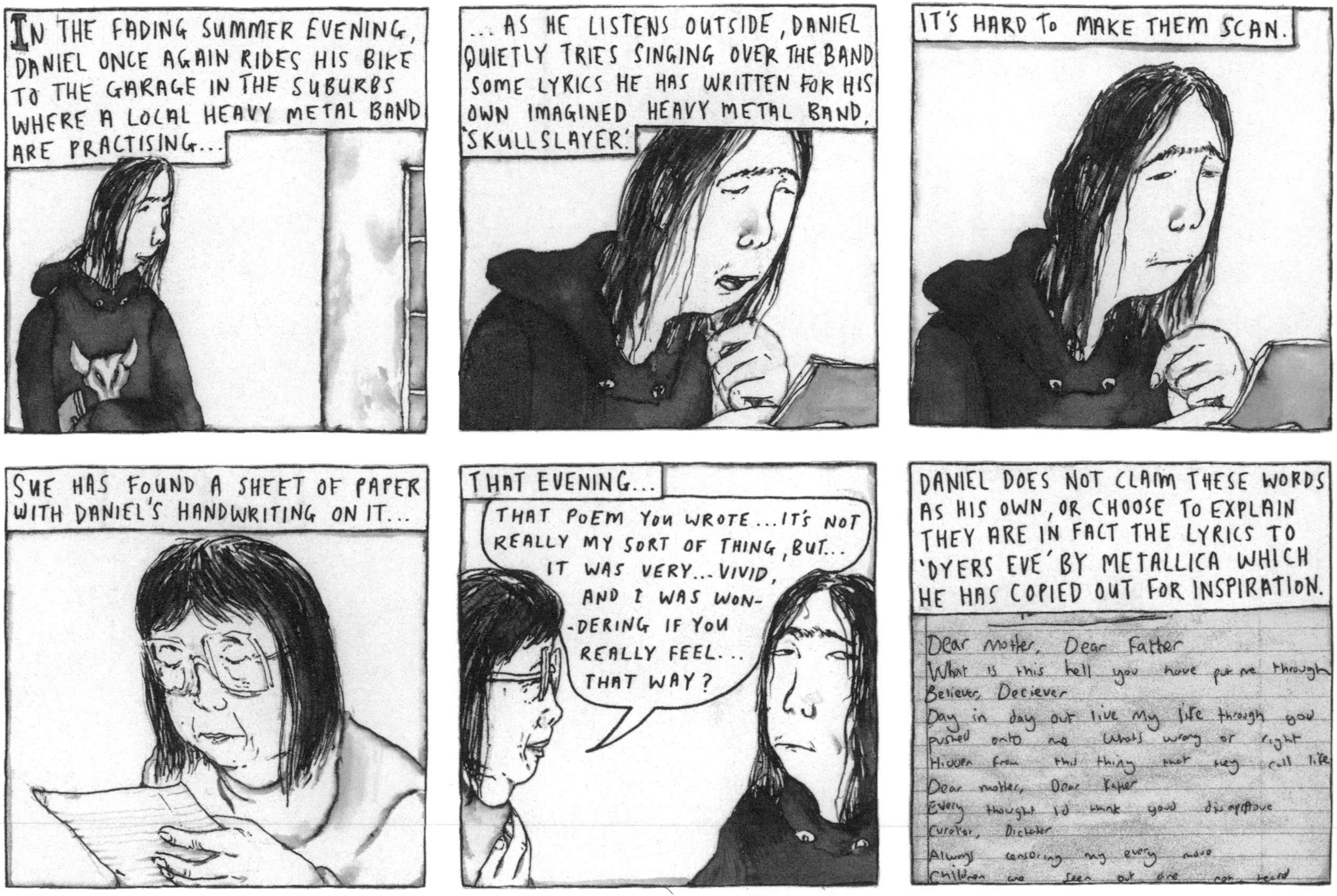
IN THE FADING SUMMER EVENING, DANIEL ONCE AGAIN RIDES HIS BIKE TO THE GARAGE IN THE SUBURBS WHERE A LOCAL HEAVY METAL BAND ARE PRACTISING...
... AS HE LISTENS OUTSIDE, DANIEL QUIETLY TRIES SINGING OVER THE BAND SOME LYRICS HE HAS WRITTEN FOR HIS OWN IMAGINED HEAVY METAL BAND, 'SKULLSLAYER.'
IT'S HARD TO MAKE THEM SCAN.
SHE HAS FOUND A SHEET OF PAPER WITH DANIEL'S HANDWRITING ON IT...
THAT EVENING...
THAT POEM YOU WROTE... IT'S NOT REALLY MY SORT OF THING, BUT... IT WAS VERY... VIVID, AND I WAS WON-DERING IF YOU REALLY FEEL... THAT WAY?
DANIEL DOES NOT CLAIM THESE WORDS AS HIS OWN, OR CHOOSE TO EXPLAIN THEY ARE IN FACT THE LYRICS TO 'DYERS EVE' BY METALLICA WHICH HE HAS COPIED OUT FOR INSPIRATION.
Dear mother, Dear Father
What is this hell you have put me through
Believer, Deciever
Day in day out live my life through you
pushed onto me whats wrong or right
Curator, Dictator
Always censoring my every move

SIGNING

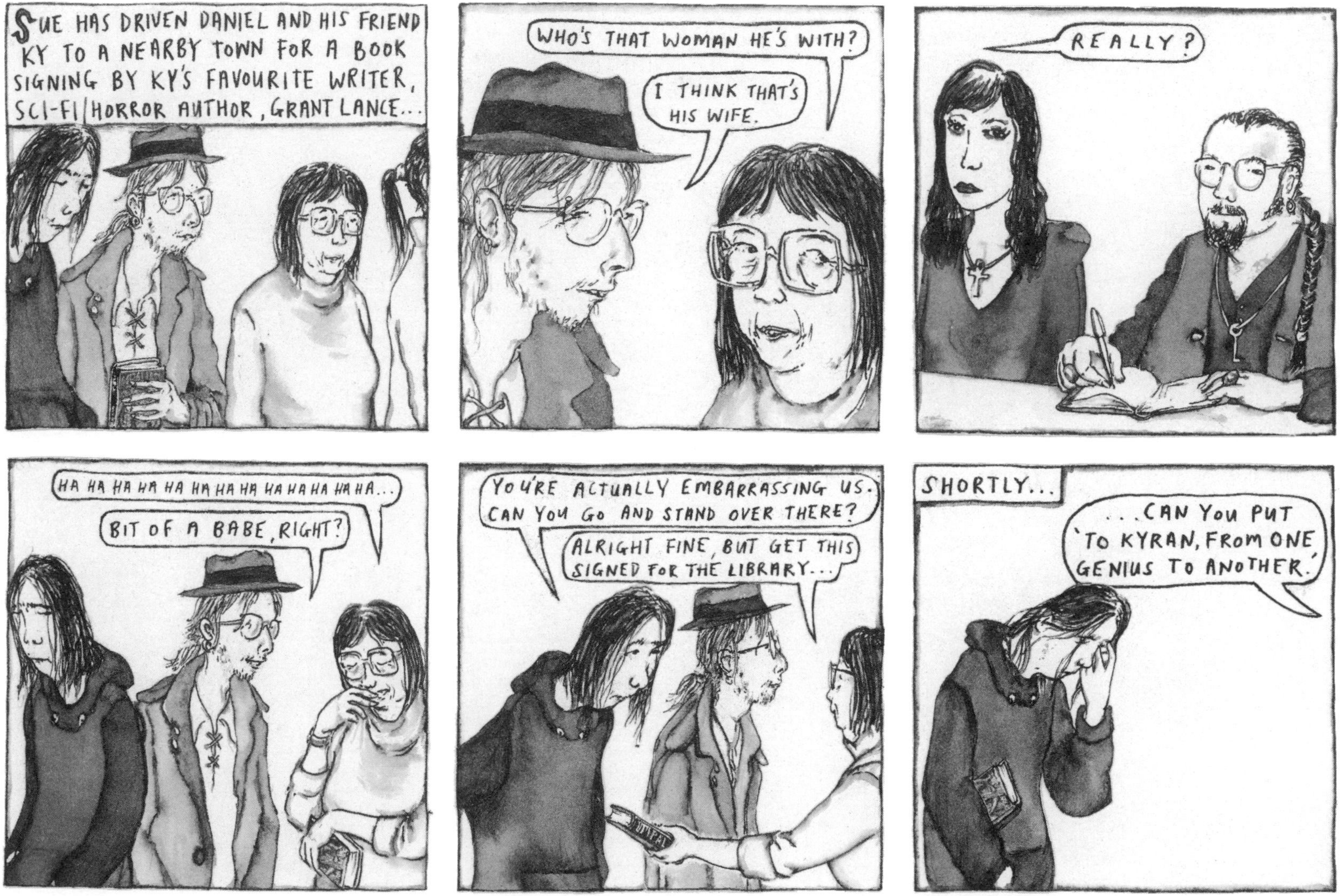
SUE HAS DRIVEN DANIEL AND HIS FRIEND KY TO A NEARBY TOWN FOR A BOOK SIGNING BY KY'S FAVOURITE WRITER, SCI-FI/HORROR AUTHOR, GRANT LANCE...
WHO'S THAT WOMAN HE'S WITH?
I THINK THAT'S HIS WIFE.
REALLY?
HA HA HA HA HA HA HA HA HA HA HA HA HA...
BIT OF A BABE, RIGHT?
YOU'RE ACTUALLY EMBARRASSING US. CAN YOU GO AND STAND OVER THERE?
ALRIGHT FINE, BUT GET THIS SIGNED FOR THE LIBRARY...
SHORTLY...
...CAN YOU PUT 'TO KYRAN, FROM ONE GENIUS TO ANOTHER.'

RESEMBLANCE

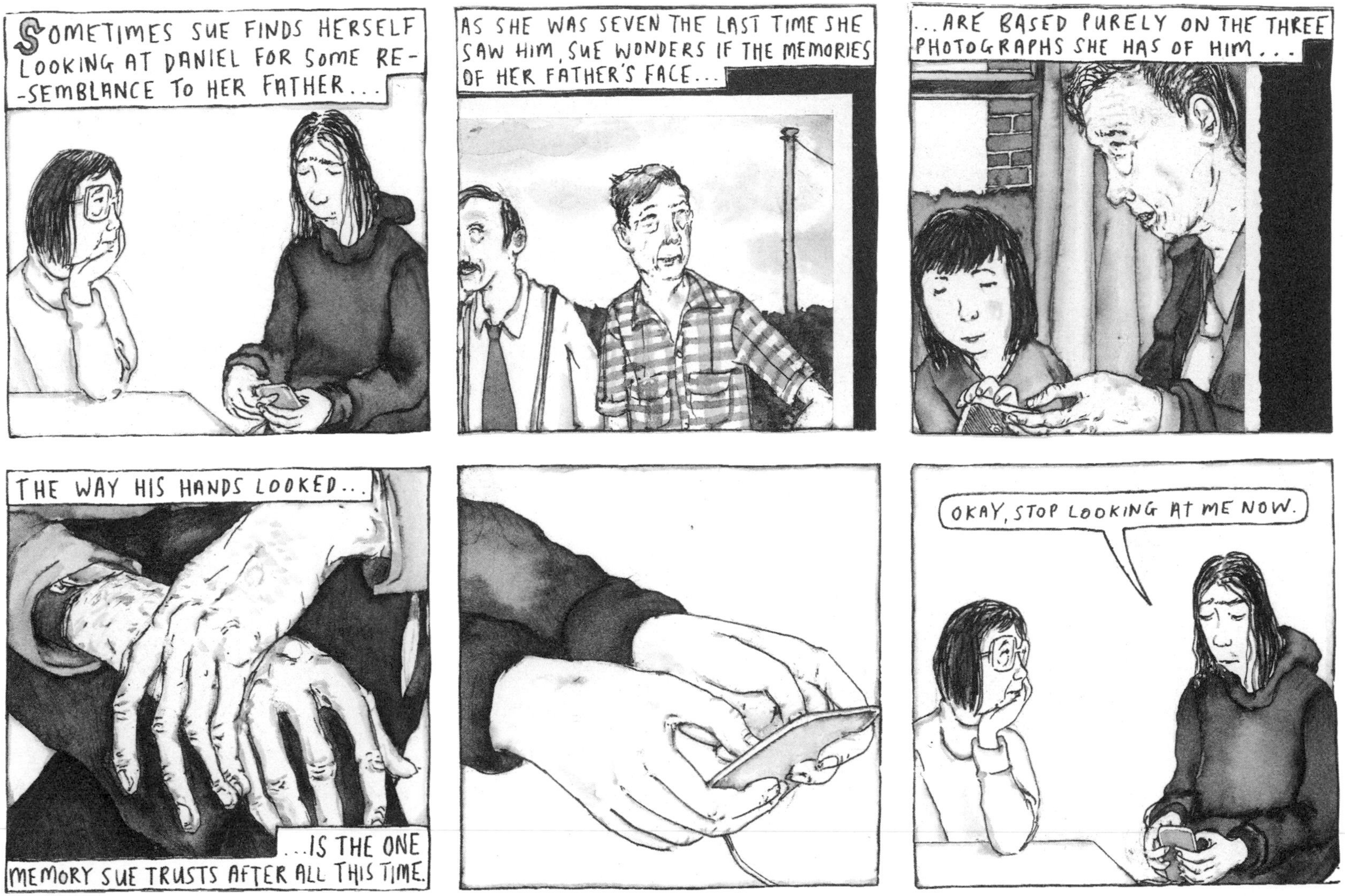
SOMETIMES SUE FINDS HERSELF LOOKING AT DANIEL FOR SOME RE-SEMBLANCE TO HER FATHER...
AS SHE WAS SEVEN THE LAST TIME SHE SAW HIM, SUE WONDERS IF THE MEMORIES OF HER FATHER'S FACE...
...ARE BASED PURELY ON THE THREE PHOTOGRAPHS SHE HAS OF HIM...
THE WAY HIS HANDS LOOKED...
...IS THE ONE MEMORY SUE TRUSTS AFTER ALL THIS TIME.
OKAY, STOP LOOKING AT ME NOW.

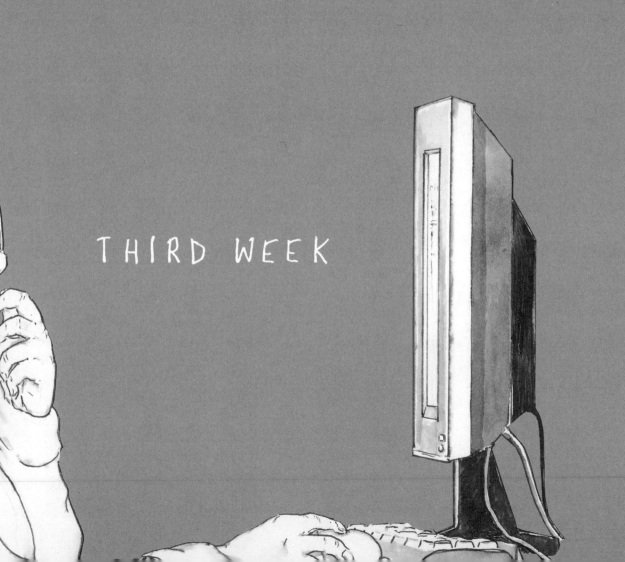

THIRD WEEK

STEREO

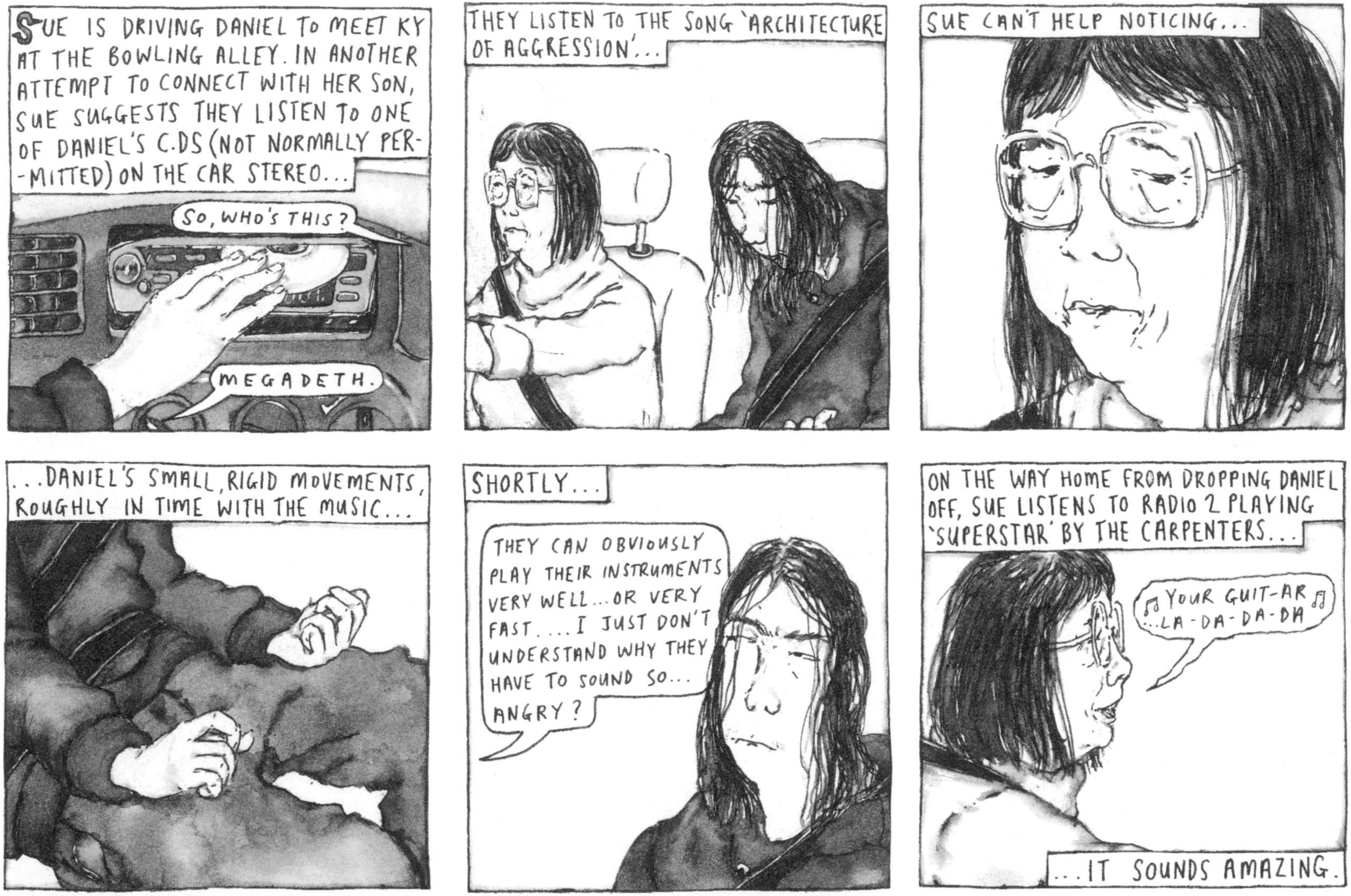
SUE IS DRIVING DANIEL TO MEET KY AT THE BOWLING ALLEY. IN ANOTHER ATTEMPT TO CONNECT WITH HER SON, SUE SUGGESTS THEY LISTEN TO ONE OF DANIEL'S C.DS (NOT NORMALLY PER-MITTED) ON THE CAR STEREO...
SO, WHO'S THIS?
MEGADETH.
THEY LISTEN TO THE SONG 'ARCHITECTURE OF AGGRESSION'...
SUE CAN'T HELP NOTICING...
...DANIEL'S SMALL, RIGID MOVEMENTS, ROUGHLY IN TIME WITH THE MUSIC...
SHORTLY...
THEY CAN OBVIOUSLY PLAY THEIR INSTRUMENTS VERY WELL...OR VERY FAST.... I JUST DON'T UNDERSTAND WHY THEY HAVE TO SOUND SO... ANGRY?
ON THE WAY HOME FROM DROPPING DANIEL OFF, SUE LISTENS TO RADIO 2 PLAYING 'SUPERSTAR' BY THE CARPENTERS...
♫ YOUR GUIT-AR ♫ ...LA-DA-DA-DA
...IT SOUNDS AMAZING.

TABLE

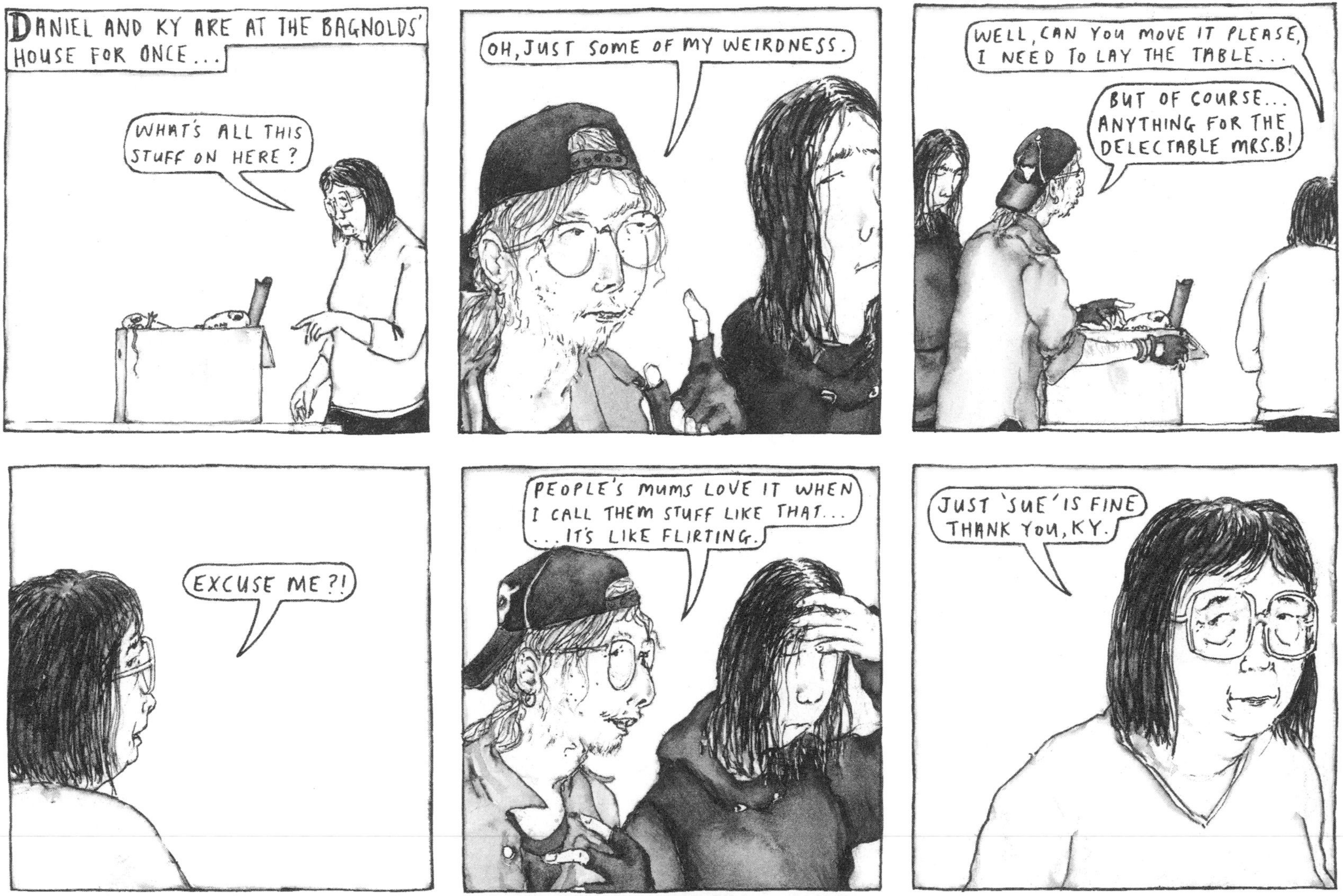
DANIEL AND KY ARE AT THE BAGNOLDS' HOUSE FOR ONCE...
WHAT'S ALL THIS STUFF ON HERE?
OH, JUST SOME OF MY WEIRDNESS.
WELL, CAN YOU MOVE IT PLEASE, I NEED TO LAY THE TABLE...
BUT OF COURSE... ANYTHING FOR THE DELECTABLE MRS. B!
EXCUSE ME?!
PEOPLE'S MUMS LOVE IT WHEN I CALL THEM STUFF LIKE THAT... ...IT'S LIKE FLIRTING.
JUST 'SUE' IS FINE THANK YOU, KY.

GUITAR

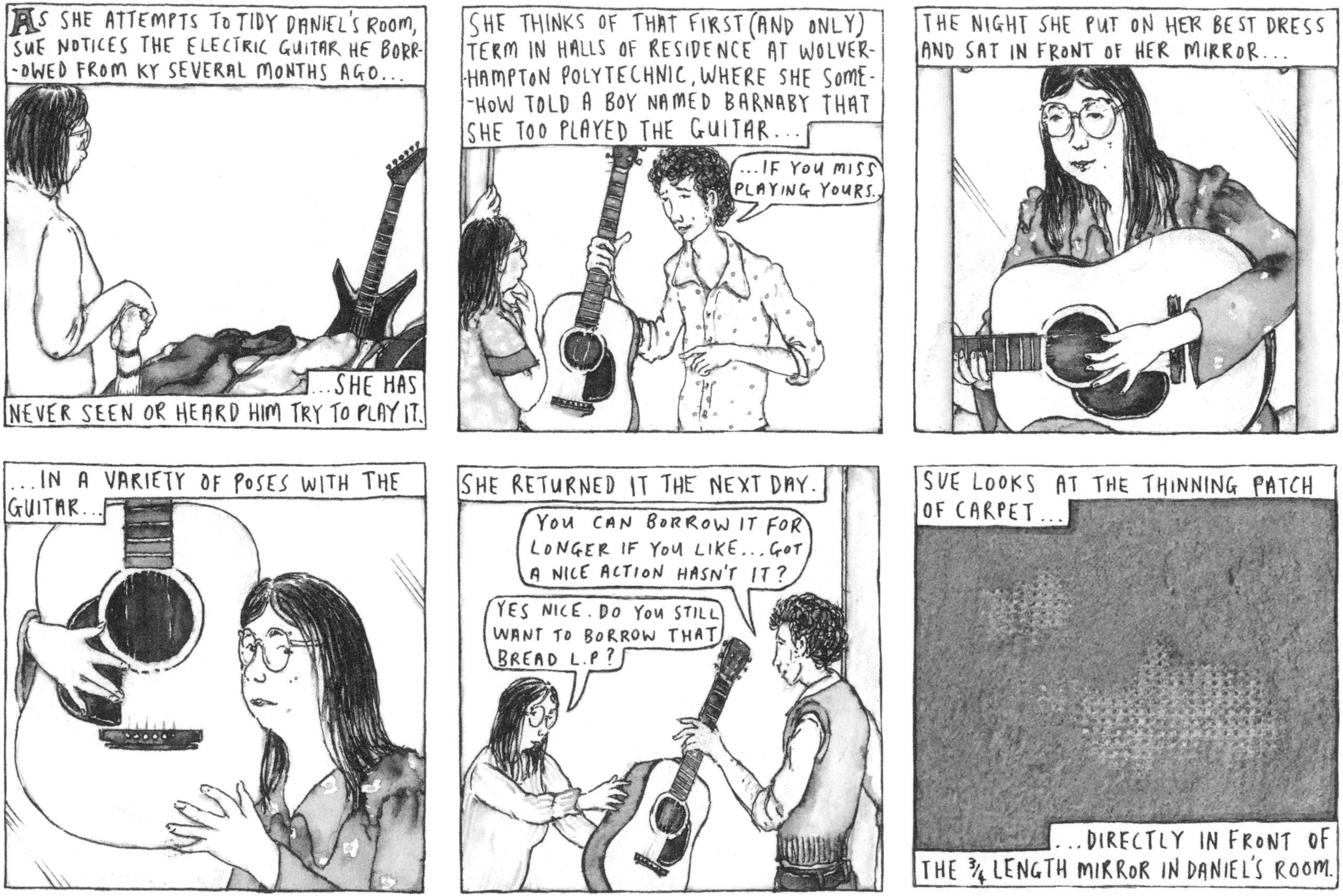

AS SHE ATTEMPTS TO TIDY DANIEL'S ROOM, SUE NOTICES THE ELECTRIC GUITAR HE BORR-OWED FROM KY SEVERAL MONTHS AGO...
...SHE HAS NEVER SEEN OR HEARD HIM TRY TO PLAY IT.
SHE THINKS OF THAT FIRST (AND ONLY) TERM IN HALLS OF RESIDENCE AT WOLVER-HAMPTON POLYTECHNIC, WHERE SHE SOME-HOW TOLD A BOY NAMED BARNABY THAT SHE TOO PLAYED THE GUITAR...
...IF YOU MISS PLAYING YOURS.
THE NIGHT SHE PUT ON HER BEST DRESS AND SAT IN FRONT OF HER MIRROR...
...IN A VARIETY OF POSES WITH THE GUITAR...
SHE RETURNED IT THE NEXT DAY.
YOU CAN BORROW IT FOR LONGER IF YOU LIKE... GOT A NICE ACTION HASN'T IT?
YES NICE. DO YOU STILL WANT TO BORROW THAT BREAD L.P?
SUE LOOKS AT THE THINNING PATCH OF CARPET...
...DIRECTLY IN FRONT OF THE 3/4 LENGTH MIRROR IN DANIEL'S ROOM.

FAMILY

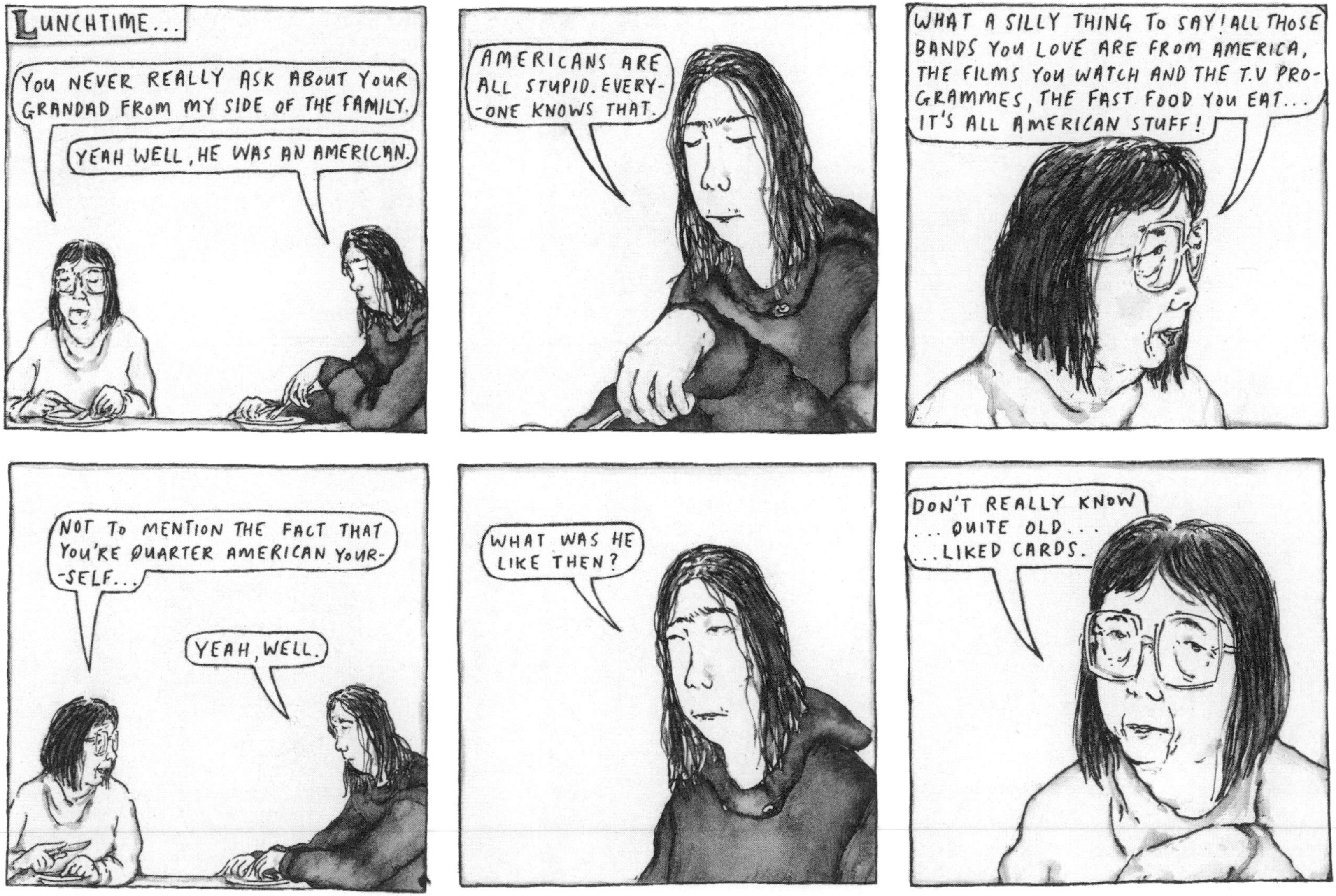
LUNCHTIME...
YOU NEVER REALLY ASK ABOUT YOUR GRANDAD FROM MY SIDE OF THE FAMILY.
YEAH WELL, HE WAS AN AMERICAN.
AMERICANS ARE ALL STUPID. EVERY-ONE KNOWS THAT.
WHAT A SILLY THING TO SAY! ALL THOSE BANDS YOU LOVE ARE FROM AMERICA, THE FILMS YOU WATCH AND THE T.V PRO-GRAMMES, THE FAST FOOD YOU EAT... IT'S ALL AMERICAN STUFF!
NOT TO MENTION THE FACT THAT YOU'RE QUARTER AMERICAN YOUR-SELF...
YEAH, WELL.
WHAT WAS HE LIKE THEN?
DON'T REALLY KNOW ...QUITE OLD... ...LIKED CARDS.

SIGNATURE

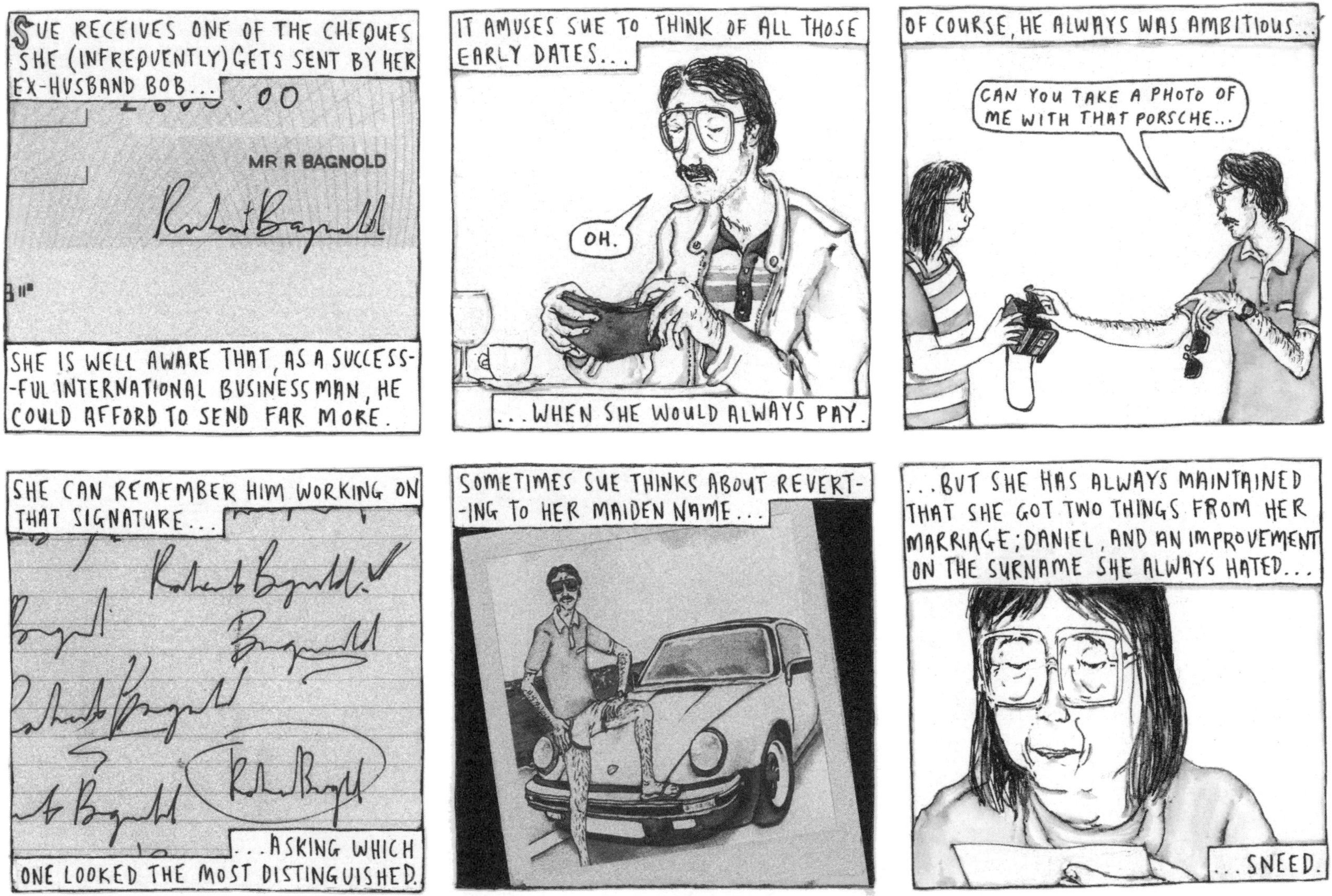
SUE RECEIVES ONE OF THE CHEQUES SHE (INFREQUENTLY) GETS SENT BY HER EX-HUSBAND BOB...
MR R BAGNOLD
SHE IS WELL AWARE THAT, AS A SUCCESS-FUL INTERNATIONAL BUSINESSMAN, HE COULD AFFORD TO SEND FAR MORE.
IT AMUSES SUE TO THINK OF ALL THOSE EARLY DATES...
OH.
...WHEN SHE WOULD ALWAYS PAY.
OF COURSE, HE ALWAYS WAS AMBITIOUS...
CAN YOU TAKE A PHOTO OF ME WITH THAT PORSCHE...
SHE CAN REMEMBER HIM WORKING ON THAT SIGNATURE...
...ASKING WHICH ONE LOOKED THE MOST DISTINGUISHED.
SOMETIMES SUE THINKS ABOUT REVERT-ING TO HER MAIDEN NAME...
...BUT SHE HAS ALWAYS MAINTAINED THAT SHE GOT TWO THINGS FROM HER MARRIAGE; DANIEL, AND AN IMPROVEMENT ON THE SURNAME SHE ALWAYS HATED...
...SNEED.

ART

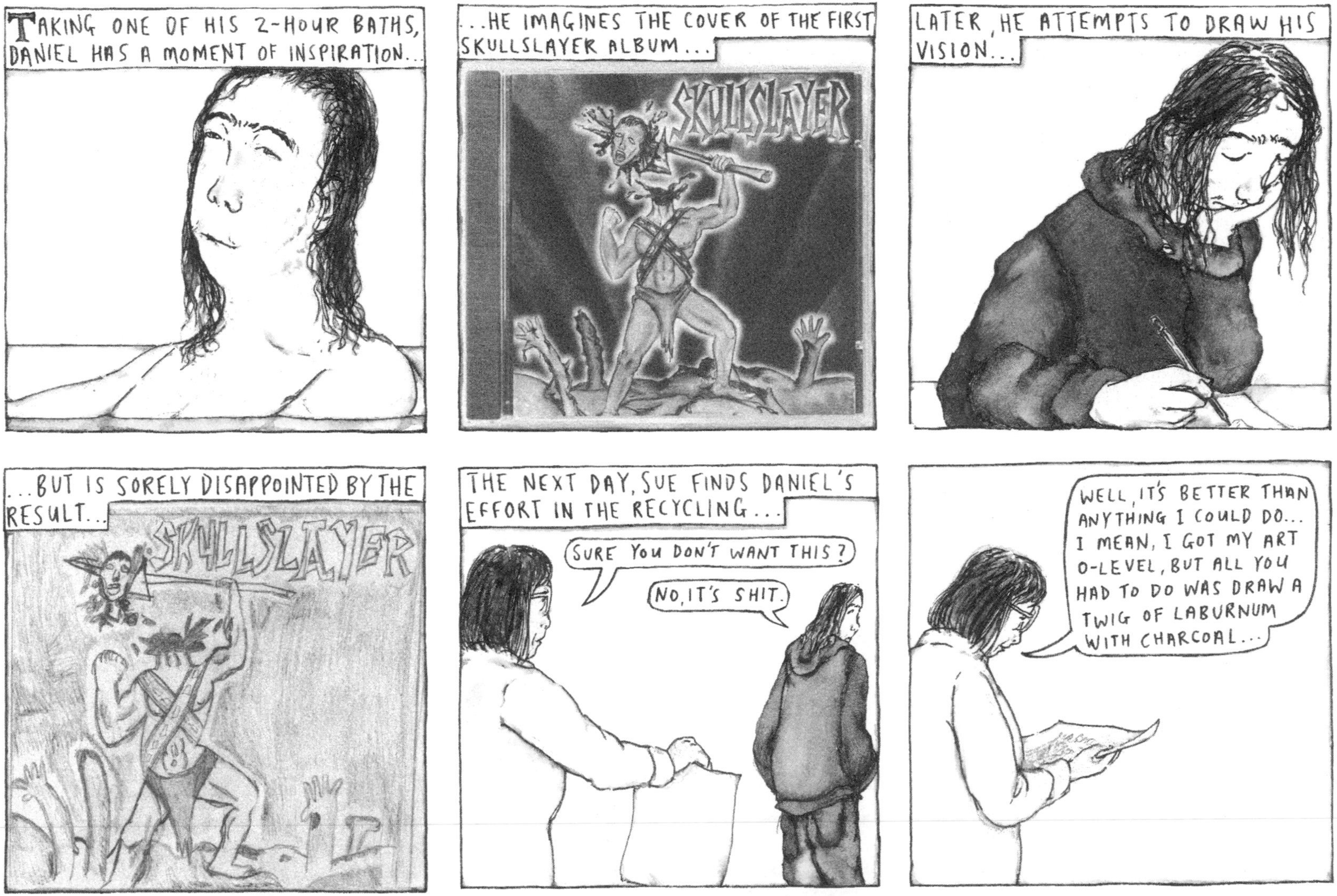
TAKING ONE OF HIS 2-HOUR BATHS, DANIEL HAS A MOMENT OF INSPIRATION...
...HE IMAGINES THE COVER OF THE FIRST SKULLSLAYER ALBUM...
SKULLSLAYER
LATER, HE ATTEMPTS TO DRAW HIS VISION...
...BUT IS SORELY DISAPPOINTED BY THE RESULT...
SKULLSLAYER
THE NEXT DAY, SUE FINDS DANIEL'S EFFORT IN THE RECYCLING...
SURE YOU DON'T WANT THIS?
NO, IT'S SHIT.
WELL, IT'S BETTER THAN ANYTHING I COULD DO... I MEAN, I GOT MY ART O-LEVEL, BUT ALL YOU HAD TO DO WAS DRAW A TWIG OF LABURNUM WITH CHARCOAL...

BABY

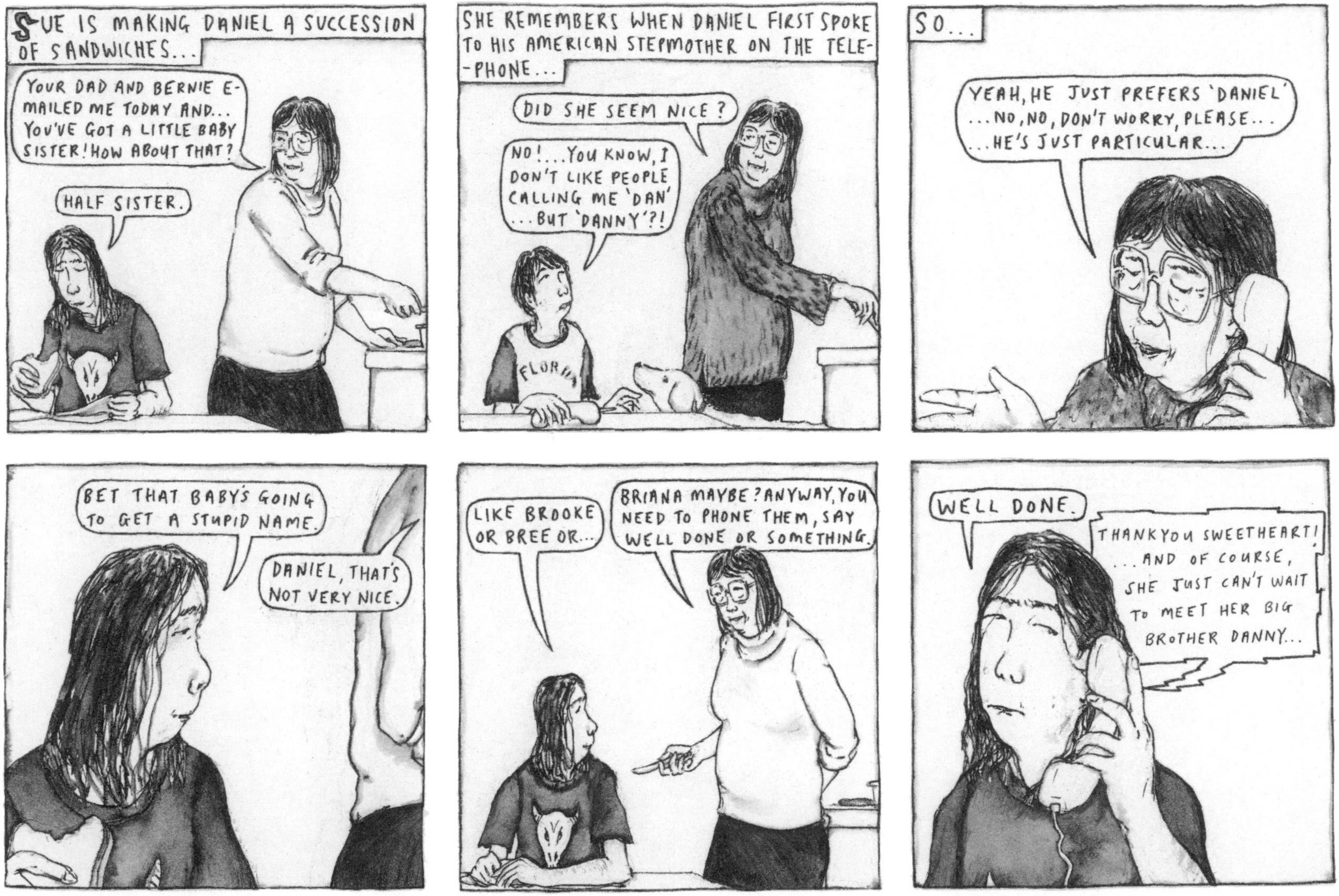
SUE IS MAKING DANIEL A SUCCESSION OF SANDWICHES...
YOUR DAD AND BERNIE E-MAILED ME TODAY AND... YOU'VE GOT A LITTLE BABY SISTER! HOW ABOUT THAT?
HALF SISTER.
SHE REMEMBERS WHEN DANIEL FIRST SPOKE TO HIS AMERICAN STEPMOTHER ON THE TELE-PHONE...
DID SHE SEEM NICE?
NO!... YOU KNOW, I DON'T LIKE PEOPLE CALLING ME 'DAN' ... BUT 'DANNY'?!
FLORIDA
SO...
YEAH, HE JUST PREFERS 'DANIEL' ...NO, NO, DON'T WORRY, PLEASE... ...HE'S JUST PARTICULAR...
BET THAT BABY'S GOING TO GET A STUPID NAME.
DANIEL, THAT'S NOT VERY NICE.
LIKE BROOKE OR BREE OR...
BRIANA MAYBE? ANYWAY, YOU NEED TO PHONE THEM, SAY WELL DONE OR SOMETHING.
WELL DONE.
THANKYOU SWEETHEART! ...AND OF COURSE, SHE JUST CAN'T WAIT TO MEET HER BIG BROTHER DANNY...

ALCOHOL

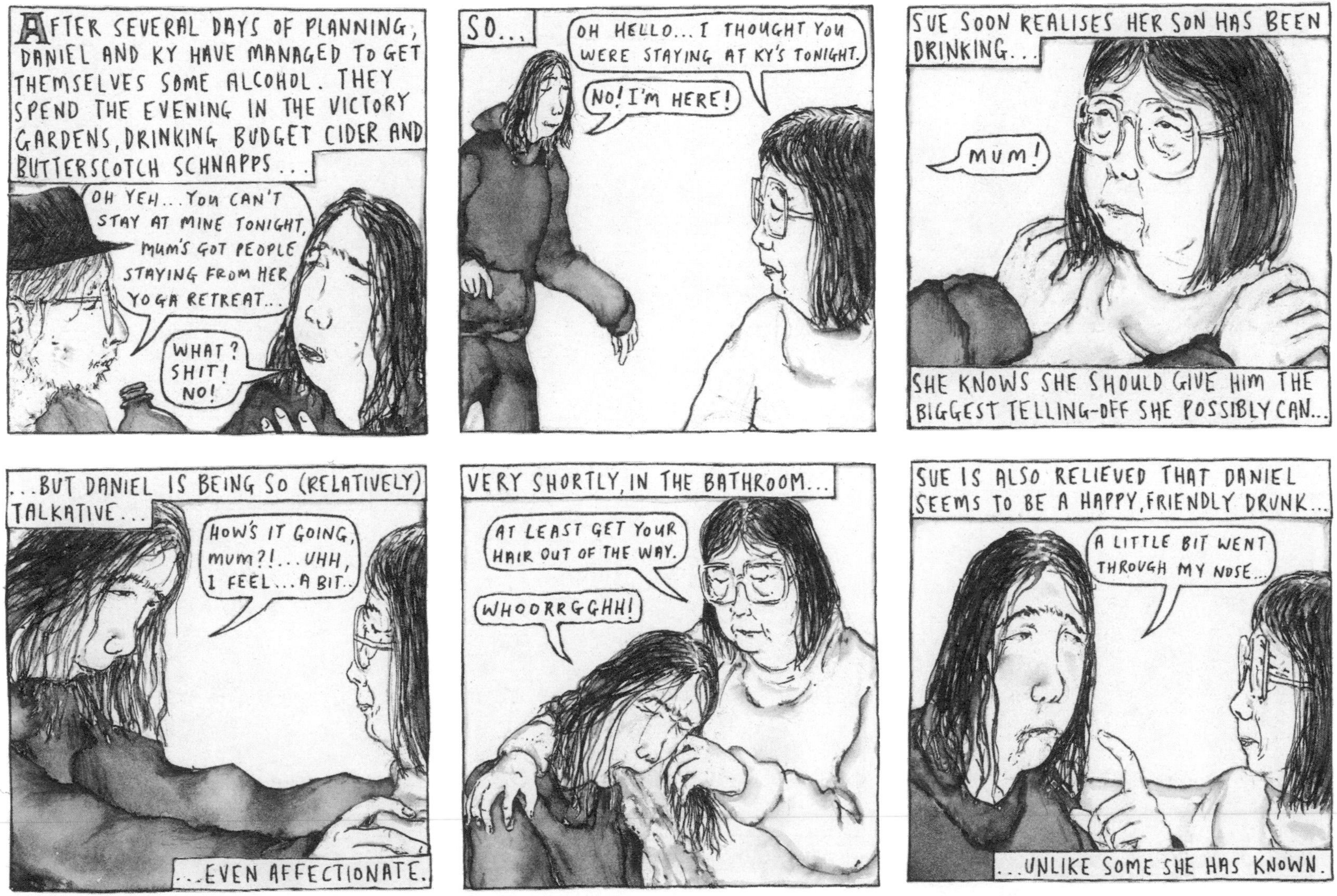
AFTER SEVERAL DAYS OF PLANNING, DANIEL AND KY HAVE MANAGED TO GET THEMSELVES SOME ALCOHOL. THEY SPEND THE EVENING IN THE VICTORY GARDENS, DRINKING BUDGET CIDER AND BUTTERSCOTCH SCHNAPPS...
OH YEH... YOU CAN'T STAY AT MINE TONIGHT, MUM'S GOT PEOPLE STAYING FROM HER YOGA RETREAT...
WHAT? SHIT! NO!
SO...
OH HELLO... I THOUGHT YOU WERE STAYING AT KY'S TONIGHT.
NO! I'M HERE!
SUE SOON REALISES HER SON HAS BEEN DRINKING...
MUM!
SHE KNOWS SHE SHOULD GIVE HIM THE BIGGEST TELLING-OFF SHE POSSIBLY CAN...
...BUT DANIEL IS BEING SO (RELATIVELY) TALKATIVE...
HOW'S IT GOING, MUM?!... UHH, I FEEL... A BIT...
...EVEN AFFECTIONATE.
VERY SHORTLY, IN THE BATHROOM...
AT LEAST GET YOUR HAIR OUT OF THE WAY.
WHOORRGGHH!
SUE IS ALSO RELIEVED THAT DANIEL SEEMS TO BE A HAPPY, FRIENDLY DRUNK...
A LITTLE BIT WENT THROUGH MY NOSE...
...UNLIKE SOME SHE HAS KNOWN.

GIRLS

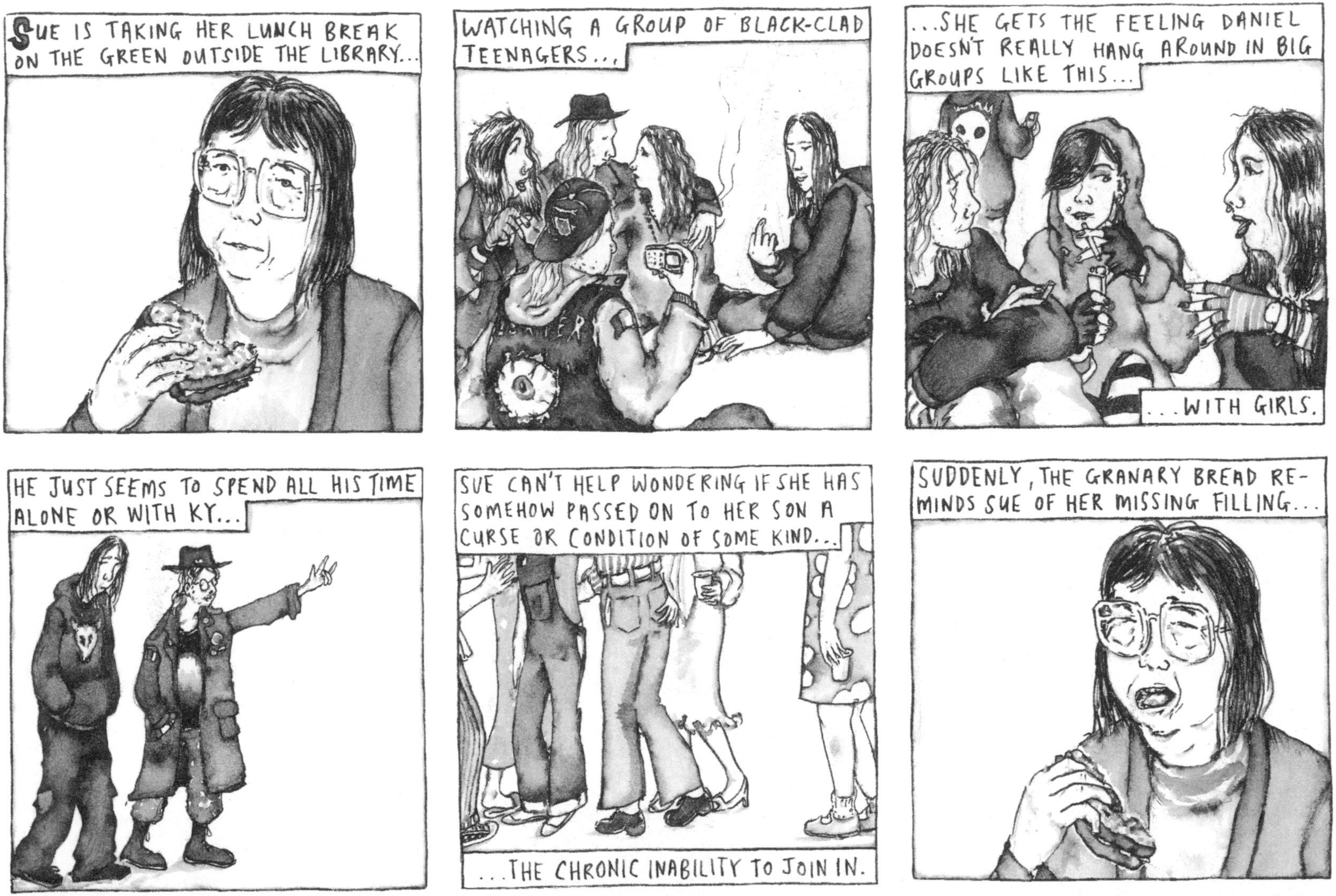
SUE IS TAKING HER LUNCH BREAK ON THE GREEN OUTSIDE THE LIBRARY...
WATCHING A GROUP OF BLACK-CLAD TEENAGERS...,
...SHE GETS THE FEELING DANIEL DOESN'T REALLY HANG AROUND IN BIG GROUPS LIKE THIS...
...WITH GIRLS.
HE JUST SEEMS TO SPEND ALL HIS TIME ALONE OR WITH KY...
SUE CAN'T HELP WONDERING IF SHE HAS SOMEHOW PASSED ON TO HER SON A CURSE OR CONDITION OF SOME KIND...
...THE CHRONIC INABILITY TO JOIN IN.
SUDDENLY, THE GRANARY BREAD RE-MINDS SUE OF HER MISSING FILLING...

T-SHIRT

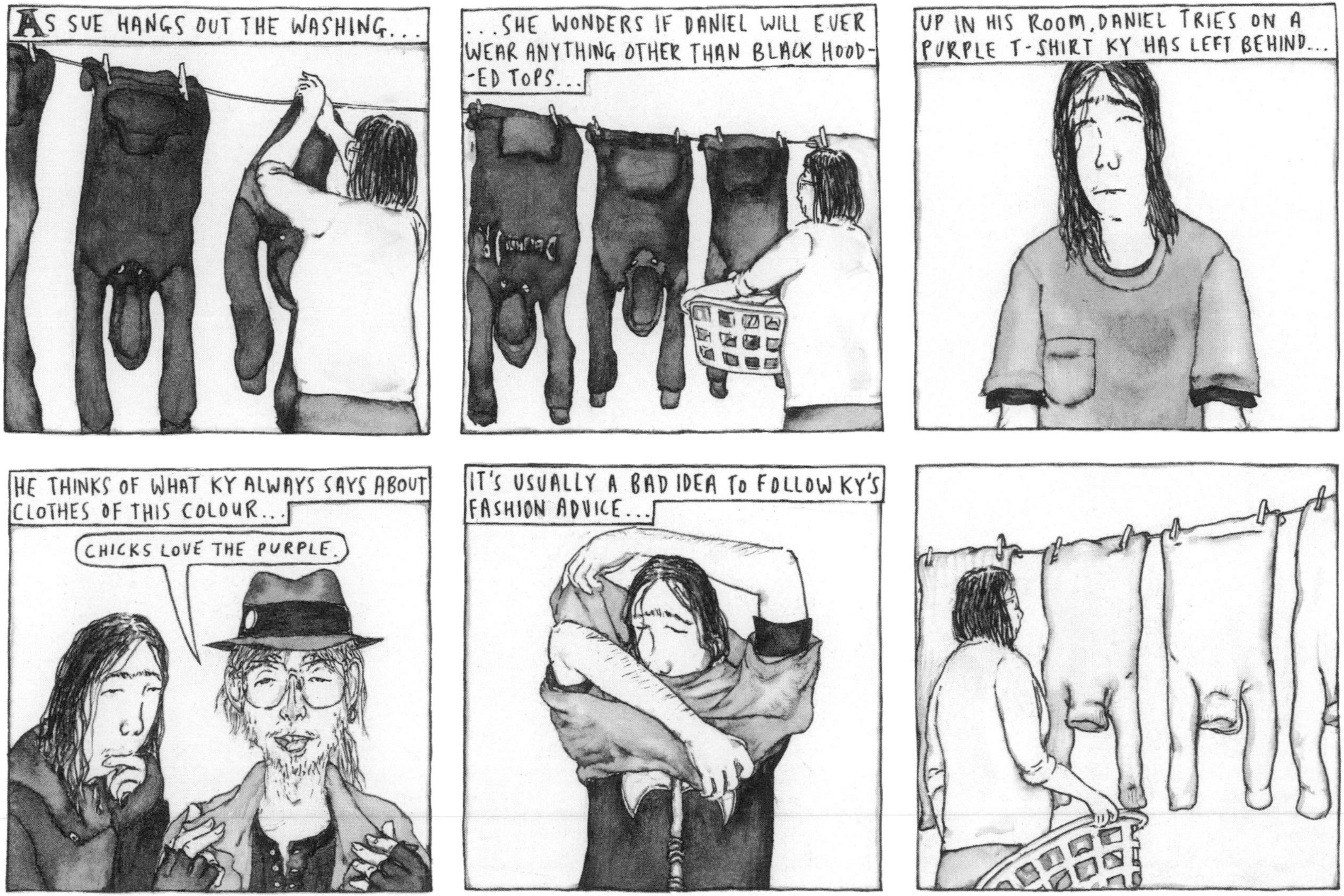
AS SUE HANGS OUT THE WASHING...
...SHE WONDERS IF DANIEL WILL EVER WEAR ANYTHING OTHER THAN BLACK HOOD-ED TOPS...
UP IN HIS ROOM, DANIEL TRIES ON A PURPLE T-SHIRT KY HAS LEFT BEHIND...
HE THINKS OF WHAT KY ALWAYS SAYS ABOUT CLOTHES OF THIS COLOUR...
CHICKS LOVE THE PURPLE.
IT'S USUALLY A BAD IDEA TO FOLLOW KY'S FASHION ADVICE...

FOURTH WEEK

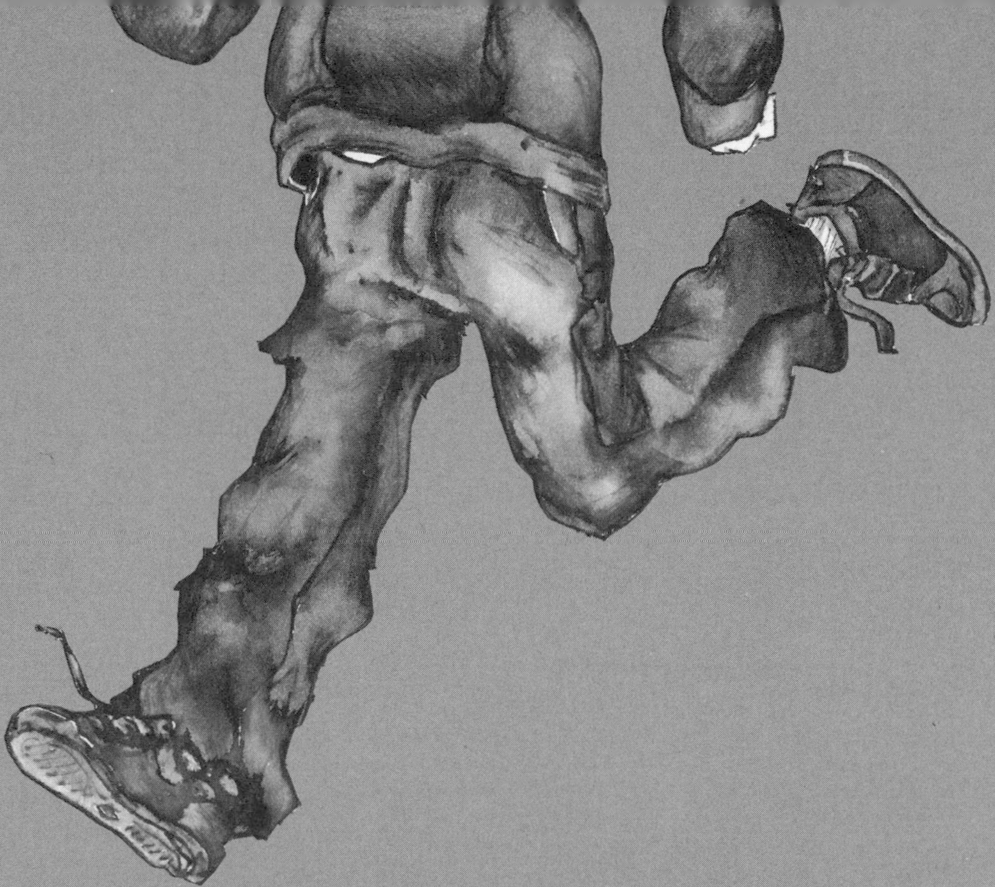

TREES

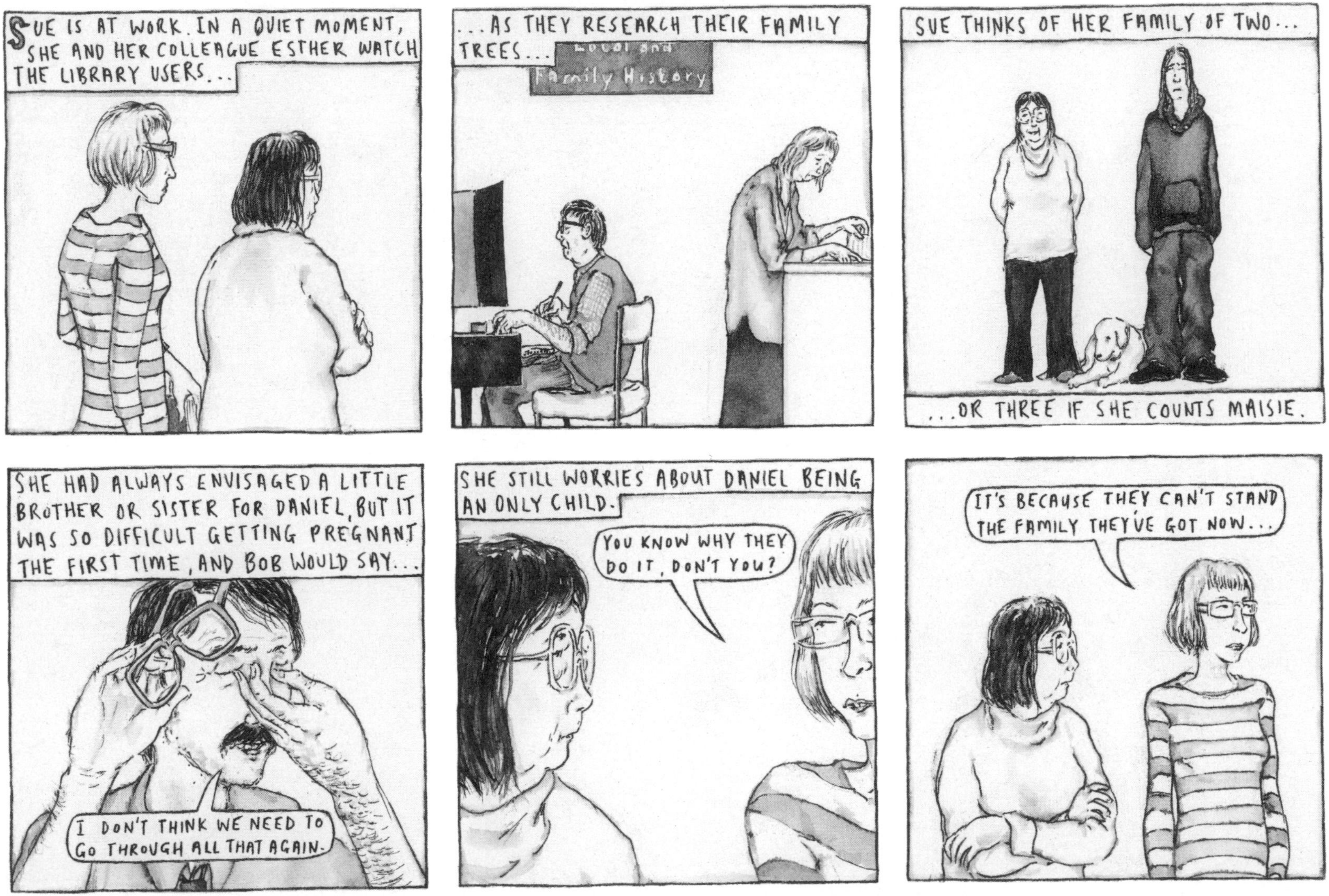
SUE IS AT WORK. IN A QUIET MOMENT, SHE AND HER COLLEAGUE ESTHER WATCH THE LIBRARY USERS...
...AS THEY RESEARCH THEIR FAMILY TREES...
Family History
SUE THINKS OF HER FAMILY OF TWO...
...OR THREE IF SHE COUNTS MAISIE.
SHE HAD ALWAYS ENVISAGED A LITTLE BROTHER OR SISTER FOR DANIEL, BUT IT WAS SO DIFFICULT GETTING PREGNANT THE FIRST TIME, AND BOB WOULD SAY...
I DON'T THINK WE NEED TO GO THROUGH ALL THAT AGAIN.
SHE STILL WORRIES ABOUT DANIEL BEING AN ONLY CHILD.
YOU KNOW WHY THEY DO IT, DON'T YOU?
IT'S BECAUSE THEY CAN'T STAND THE FAMILY THEY'VE GOT NOW...

MESS

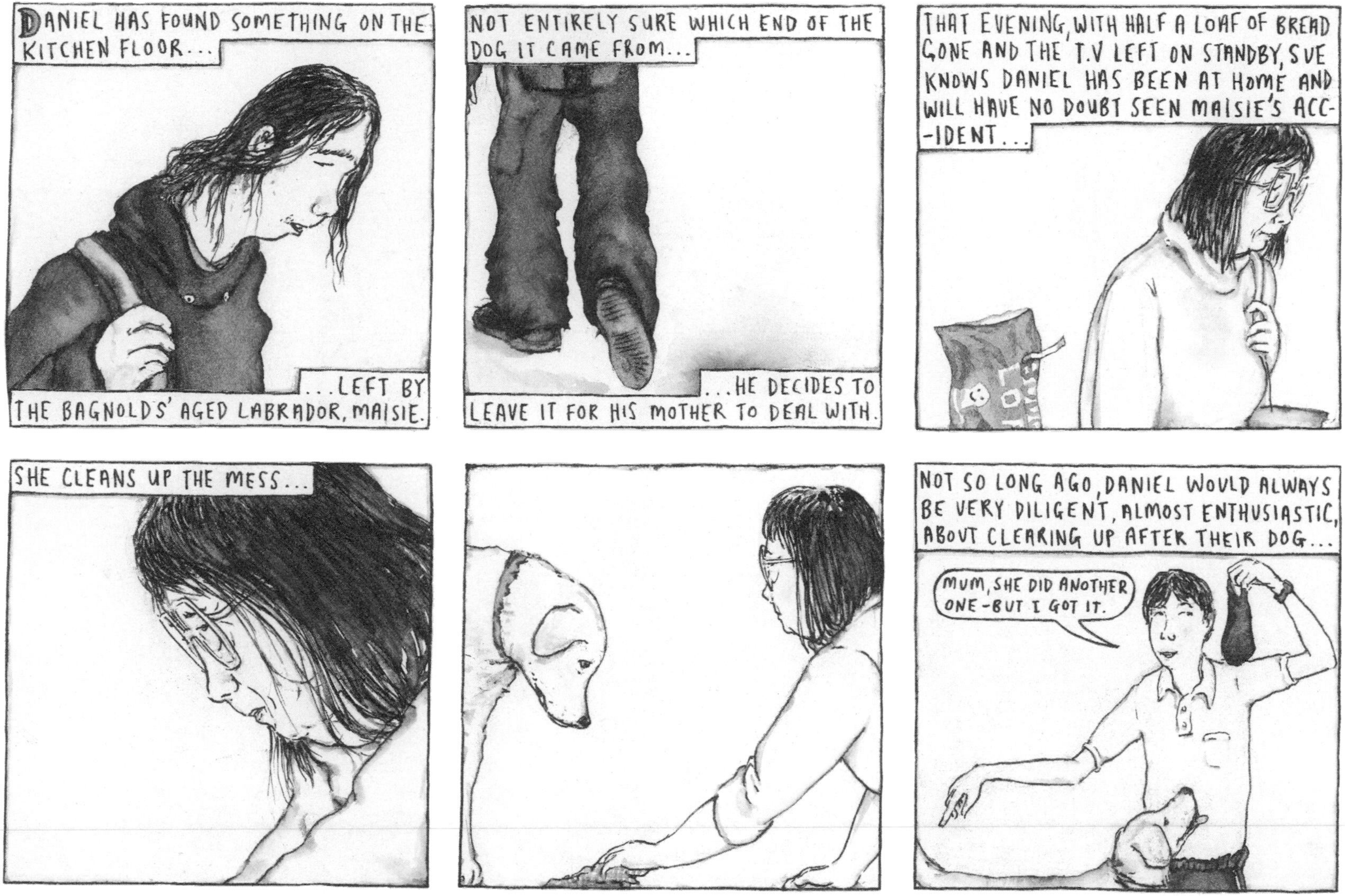
DANIEL HAS FOUND SOMETHING ON THE KITCHEN FLOOR...
...LEFT BY THE BAGNOLDS' AGED LABRADOR, MAISIE.
NOT ENTIRELY SURE WHICH END OF THE DOG IT CAME FROM...
...HE DECIDES TO LEAVE IT FOR HIS MOTHER TO DEAL WITH.
THAT EVENING, WITH HALF A LOAF OF BREAD GONE AND THE T.V LEFT ON STANDBY, SUE KNOWS DANIEL HAS BEEN AT HOME AND WILL HAVE NO DOUBT SEEN MAISIE'S ACC--IDENT...
SHE CLEANS UP THE MESS...
NOT SO LONG AGO, DANIEL WOULD ALWAYS BE VERY DILIGENT, ALMOST ENTHUSIASTIC, ABOUT CLEARING UP AFTER THEIR DOG...
MUM, SHE DID ANOTHER ONE - BUT I GOT IT.

LONG

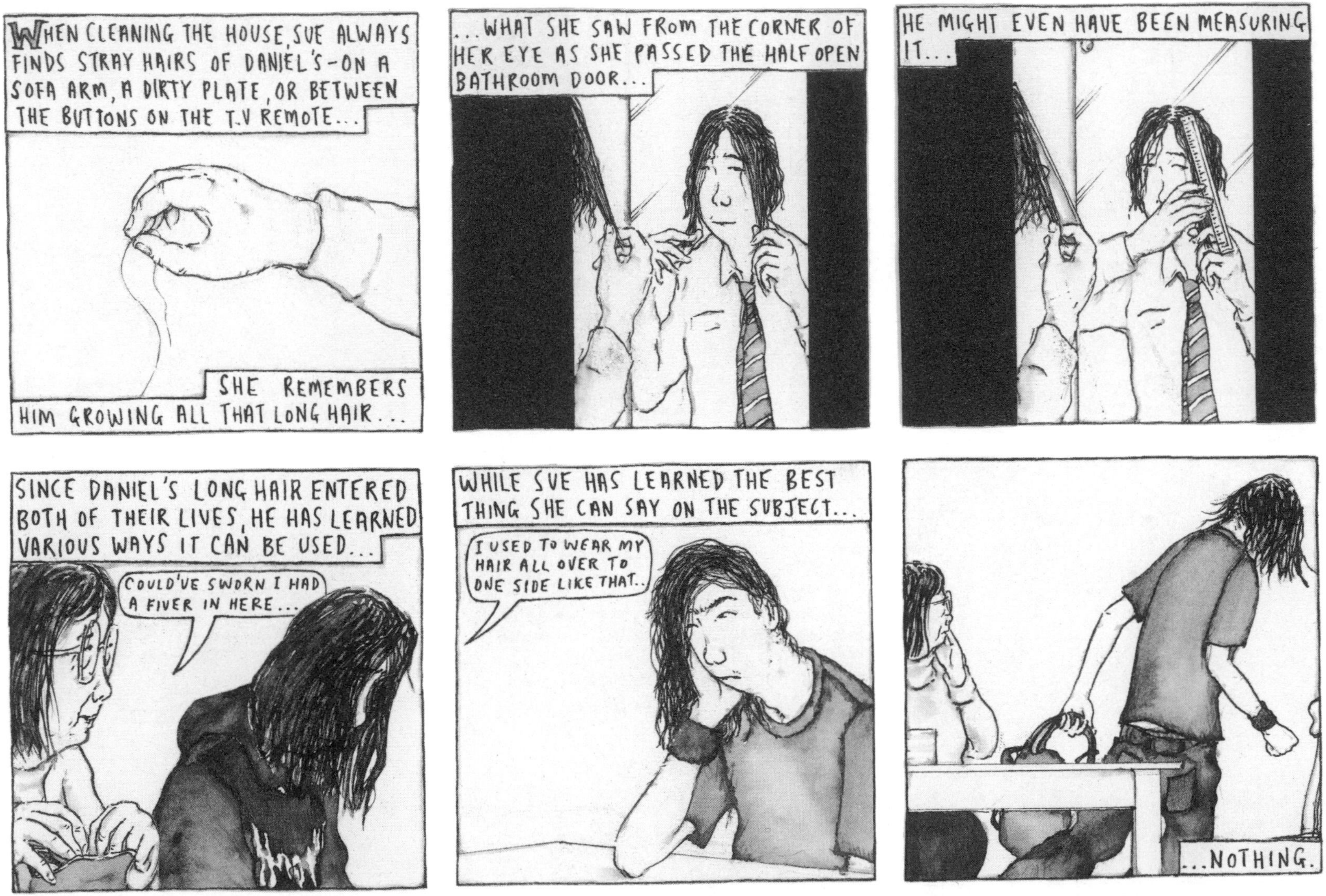
WHEN CLEANING THE HOUSE, SUE ALWAYS FINDS STRAY HAIRS OF DANIEL'S - ON A SOFA ARM, A DIRTY PLATE, OR BETWEEN THE BUTTONS ON THE T.V REMOTE...
SHE REMEMBERS HIM GROWING ALL THAT LONG HAIR...
...WHAT SHE SAW FROM THE CORNER OF HER EYE AS SHE PASSED THE HALF OPEN BATHROOM DOOR...
HE MIGHT EVEN HAVE BEEN MEASURING IT...
SINCE DANIEL'S LONG HAIR ENTERED BOTH OF THEIR LIVES, HE HAS LEARNED VARIOUS WAYS IT CAN BE USED...
COULD'VE SWORN I HAD A FIVER IN HERE...
WHILE SUE HAS LEARNED THE BEST THING SHE CAN SAY ON THE SUBJECT...
I USED TO WEAR MY HAIR ALL OVER TO ONE SIDE LIKE THAT..
...NOTHING.

HOT

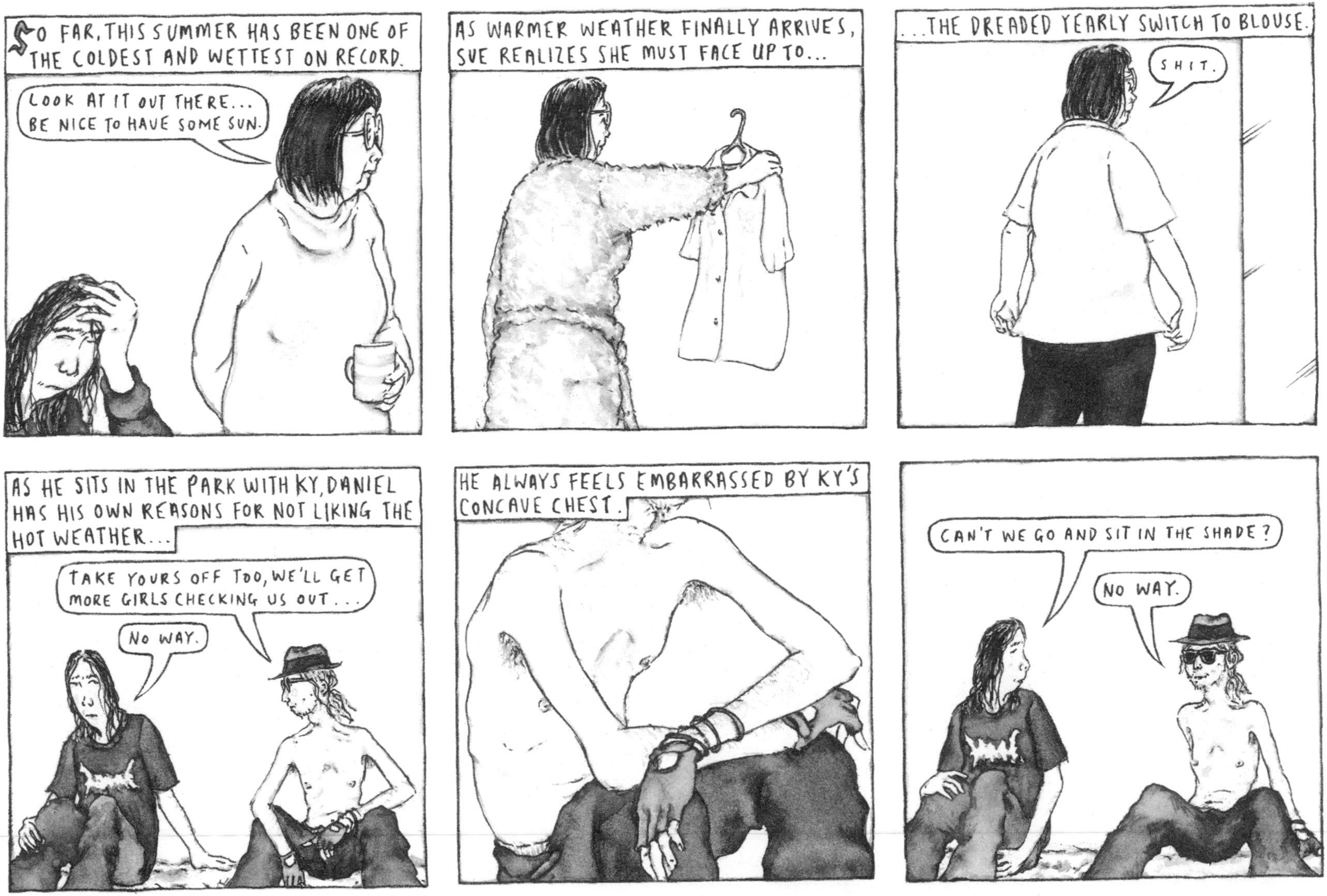
SO FAR, THIS SUMMER HAS BEEN ONE OF THE COLDEST AND WETTEST ON RECORD.
LOOK AT IT OUT THERE... BE NICE TO HAVE SOME SUN.
AS WARMER WEATHER FINALLY ARRIVES, SUE REALIZES SHE MUST FACE UP TO...
...THE DREADED YEARLY SWITCH TO BLOUSE.
SHIT.
AS HE SITS IN THE PARK WITH KY, DANIEL HAS HIS OWN REASONS FOR NOT LIKING THE HOT WEATHER...
TAKE YOURS OFF TOO, WE'LL GET MORE GIRLS CHECKING US OUT...
NO WAY.
HE ALWAYS FEELS EMBARRASSED BY KY'S CONCAVE CHEST.
CAN'T WE GO AND SIT IN THE SHADE?
NO WAY.

NIGHT

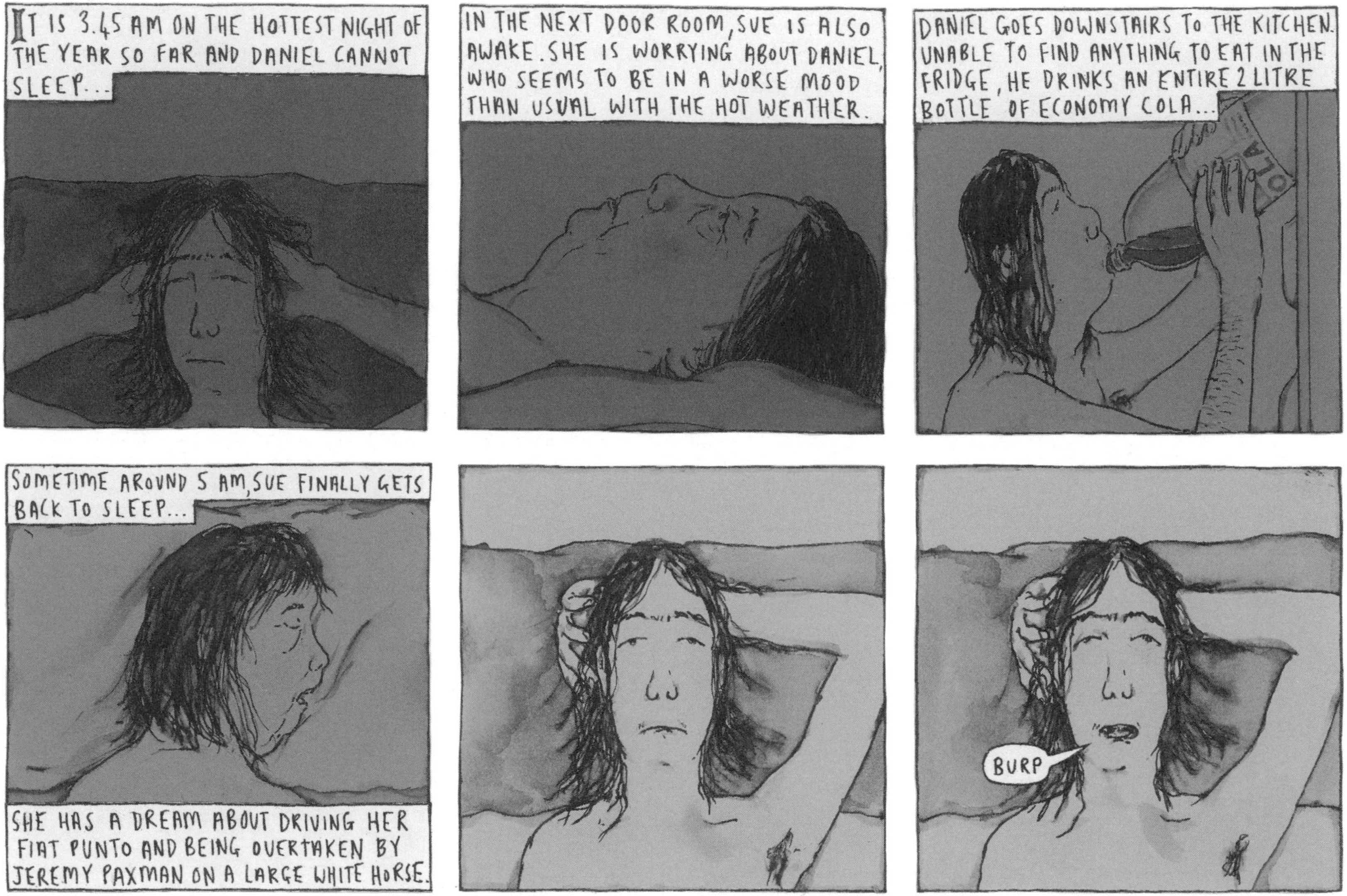

IT IS 3.45 AM ON THE HOTTEST NIGHT OF THE YEAR SO FAR AND DANIEL CANNOT SLEEP...
IN THE NEXT DOOR ROOM, SUE IS ALSO AWAKE. SHE IS WORRYING ABOUT DANIEL, WHO SEEMS TO BE IN A WORSE MOOD THAN USUAL WITH THE HOT WEATHER.
DANIEL GOES DOWNSTAIRS TO THE KITCHEN. UNABLE TO FIND ANYTHING TO EAT IN THE FRIDGE, HE DRINKS AN ENTIRE 2 LITRE BOTTLE OF ECONOMY COLA...
COLA
SOMETIME AROUND 5 AM, SUE FINALLY GETS BACK TO SLEEP...
SHE HAS A DREAM ABOUT DRIVING HER FIAT PUNTO AND BEING OVERTAKEN BY JEREMY PAXMAN ON A LARGE WHITE HORSE.
BURP

GAME

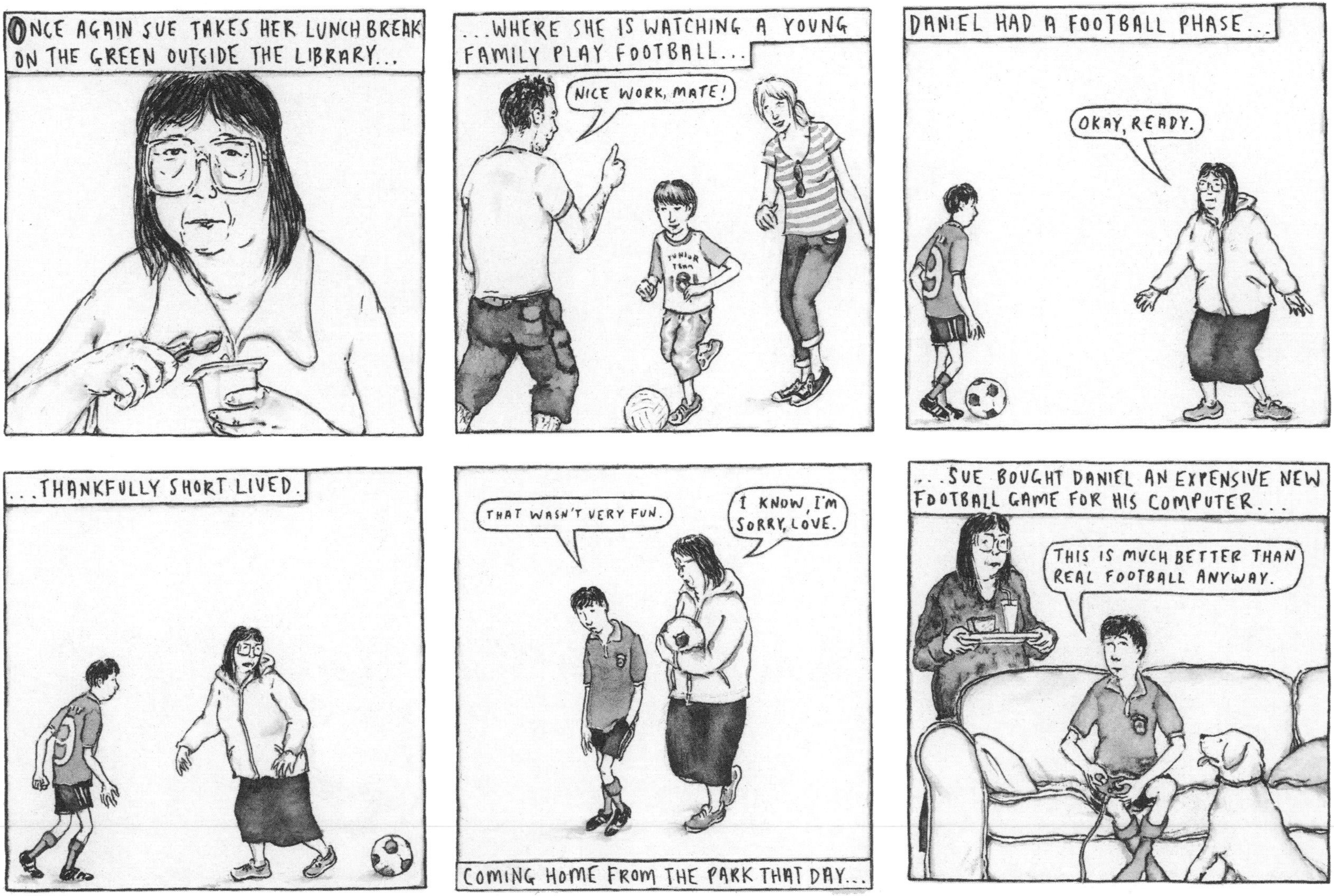
ONCE AGAIN SUE TAKES HER LUNCH BREAK ON THE GREEN OUTSIDE THE LIBRARY...
...WHERE SHE IS WATCHING A YOUNG FAMILY PLAY FOOTBALL...
NICE WORK, MATE!
DANIEL HAD A FOOTBALL PHASE...
OKAY, READY.
...THANKFULLY SHORT LIVED.
THAT WASN'T VERY FUN.
I KNOW, I'M SORRY, LOVE.
COMING HOME FROM THE PARK THAT DAY...
...SUE BOUGHT DANIEL AN EXPENSIVE NEW FOOTBALL GAME FOR HIS COMPUTER...
THIS IS MUCH BETTER THAN REAL FOOTBALL ANYWAY.

WINNING

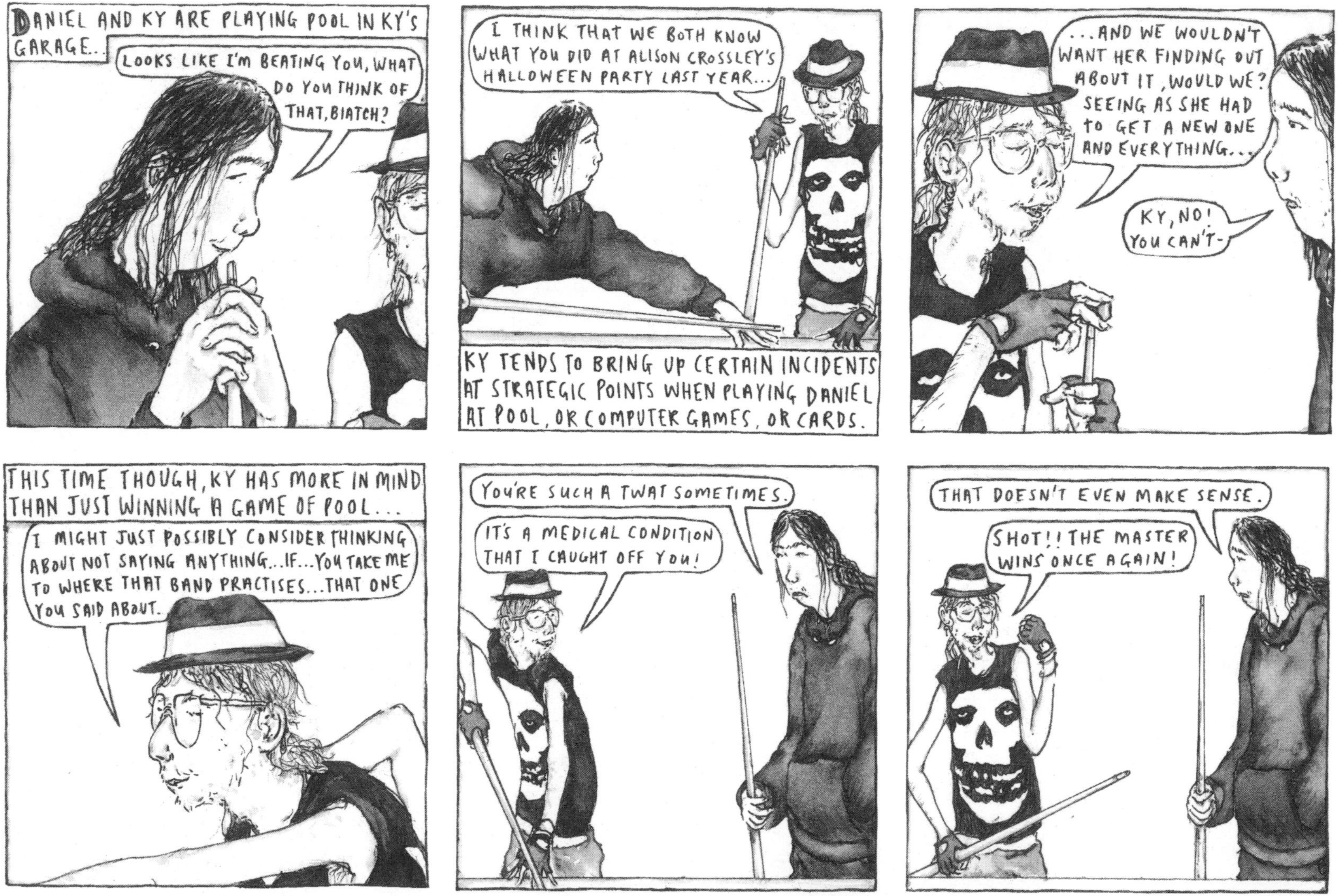
DANIEL AND KY ARE PLAYING POOL IN KY'S GARAGE..
LOOKS LIKE I'M BEATING YOU, WHAT DO YOU THINK OF THAT, BIATCH?
I THINK THAT WE BOTH KNOW WHAT YOU DID AT ALISON CROSSLEY'S HALLOWEEN PARTY LAST YEAR...
KY TENDS TO BRING UP CERTAIN INCIDENTS AT STRATEGIC POINTS WHEN PLAYING DANIEL AT POOL, OR COMPUTER GAMES, OR CARDS.
...AND WE WOULDN'T WANT HER FINDING OUT ABOUT IT, WOULD WE? SEEING AS SHE HAD TO GET A NEW ONE AND EVERYTHING...
KY, NO! YOU CAN'T-
THIS TIME THOUGH, KY HAS MORE IN MIND THAN JUST WINNING A GAME OF POOL...
I MIGHT JUST POSSIBLY CONSIDER THINKING ABOUT NOT SAYING ANYTHING...IF...YOU TAKE ME TO WHERE THAT BAND PRACTISES...THAT ONE YOU SAID ABOUT.
YOU'RE SUCH A TWAT SOMETIMES.
IT'S A MEDICAL CONDITION THAT I CAUGHT OFF YOU!
THAT DOESN'T EVEN MAKE SENSE.
SHOT!! THE MASTER WINS ONCE AGAIN!

FRIEND

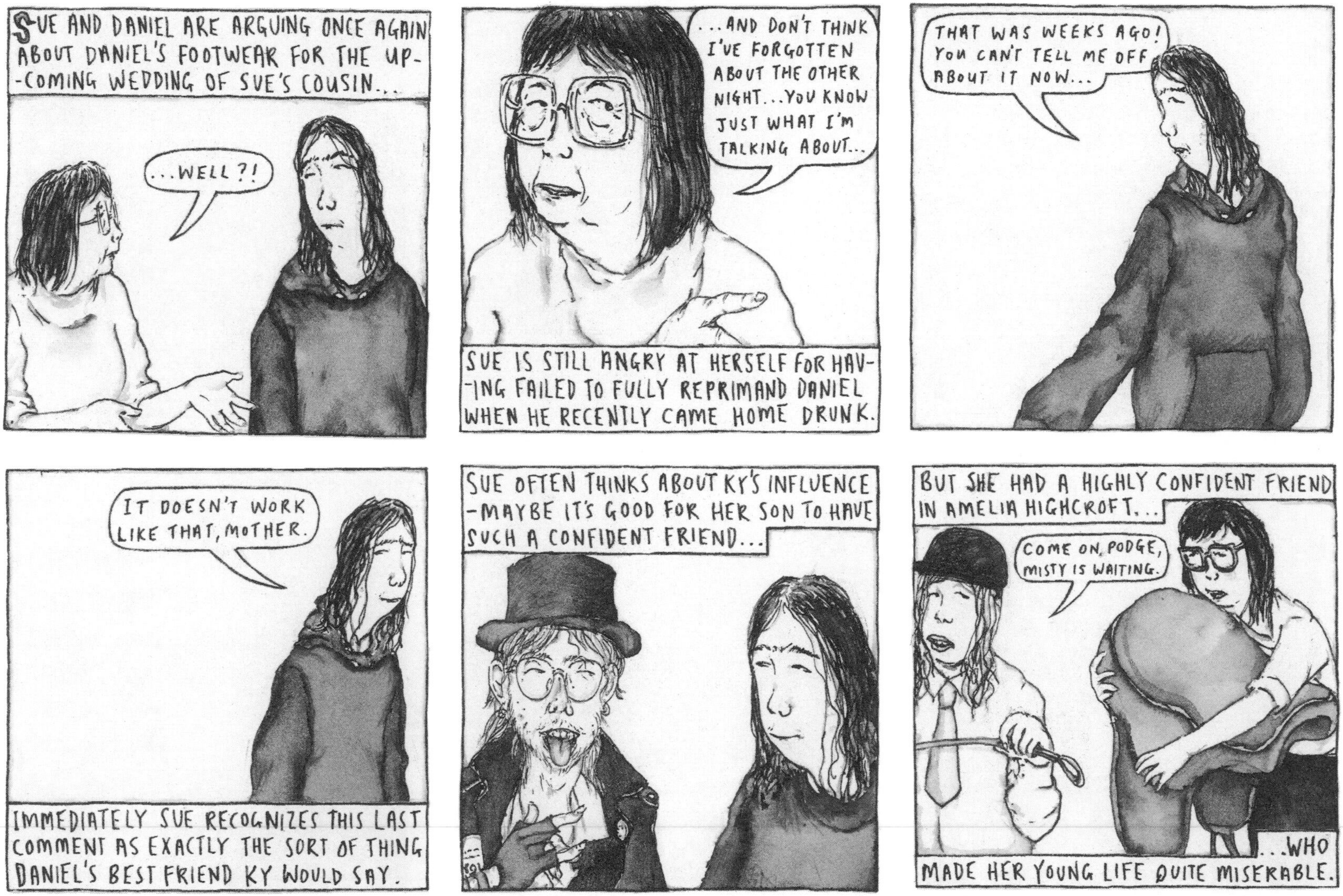
SUE AND DANIEL ARE ARGUING ONCE AGAIN ABOUT DANIEL'S FOOTWEAR FOR THE UP-COMING WEDDING OF SUE'S COUSIN...
...WELL?!
...AND DON'T THINK I'VE FORGOTTEN ABOUT THE OTHER NIGHT...YOU KNOW JUST WHAT I'M TALKING ABOUT...
SUE IS STILL ANGRY AT HERSELF FOR HAV-ING FAILED TO FULLY REPRIMAND DANIEL WHEN HE RECENTLY CAME HOME DRUNK.
THAT WAS WEEKS AGO! YOU CAN'T TELL ME OFF ABOUT IT NOW...
IT DOESN'T WORK LIKE THAT, MOTHER.
IMMEDIATELY SUE RECOGNIZES THIS LAST COMMENT AS EXACTLY THE SORT OF THING DANIEL'S BEST FRIEND KY WOULD SAY.
SUE OFTEN THINKS ABOUT KY'S INFLUENCE -MAYBE IT'S GOOD FOR HER SON TO HAVE SUCH A CONFIDENT FRIEND...
BUT SHE HAD A HIGHLY CONFIDENT FRIEND IN AMELIA HIGHCROFT...
COME ON, PODGE, MISTY IS WAITING.
...WHO MADE HER YOUNG LIFE QUITE MISERABLE.

PACKAGE

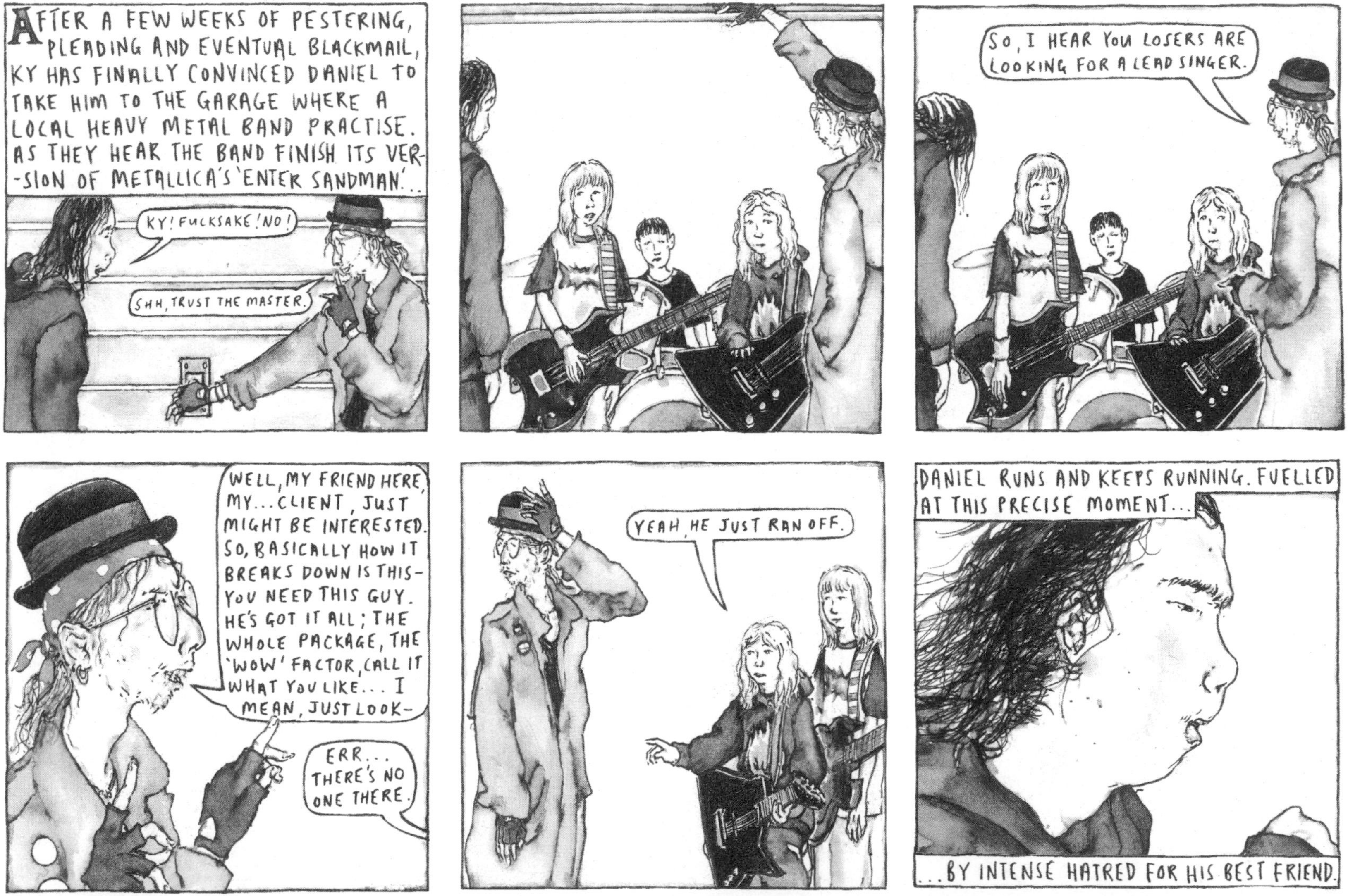

AFTER A FEW WEEKS OF PESTERING, PLEADING AND EVENTUAL BLACKMAIL, KY HAS FINALLY CONVINCED DANIEL TO TAKE HIM TO THE GARAGE WHERE A LOCAL HEAVY METAL BAND PRACTISE. AS THEY HEAR THE BAND FINISH ITS VER-SION OF METALLICA'S 'ENTER SANDMAN'...
KY! FUCKSAKE! NO!
SHH, TRUST THE MASTER.
SO, I HEAR YOU LOSERS ARE LOOKING FOR A LEAD SINGER.
WELL, MY FRIEND HERE, MY... CLIENT, JUST MIGHT BE INTERESTED. SO, BASICALLY HOW IT BREAKS DOWN IS THIS- YOU NEED THIS GUY. HE'S GOT IT ALL; THE WHOLE PACKAGE, THE 'WOW' FACTOR, CALL IT WHAT YOU LIKE... I MEAN, JUST LOOK-
ERR... THERE'S NO ONE THERE.
YEAH, HE JUST RAN OFF.
DANIEL RUNS AND KEEPS RUNNING. FUELLED AT THIS PRECISE MOMENT...
...BY INTENSE HATRED FOR HIS BEST FRIEND.

FIFTH WEEK

TELLING

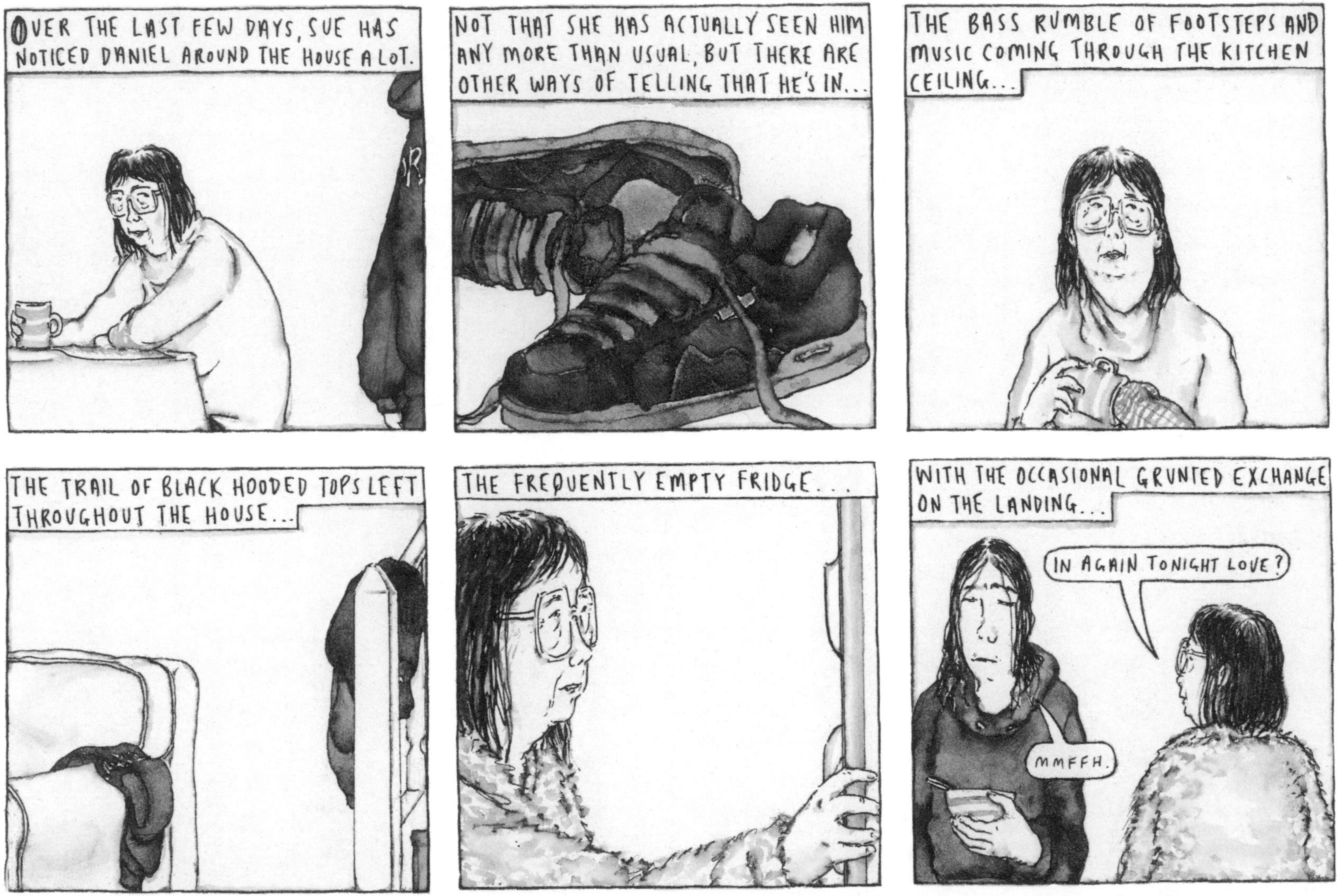
OVER THE LAST FEW DAYS, SUE HAS NOTICED DANIEL AROUND THE HOUSE A LOT.
NOT THAT SHE HAS ACTUALLY SEEN HIM ANY MORE THAN USUAL, BUT THERE ARE OTHER WAYS OF TELLING THAT HE'S IN...
THE BASS RUMBLE OF FOOTSTEPS AND MUSIC COMING THROUGH THE KITCHEN CEILING...
THE TRAIL OF BLACK HOODED TOPS LEFT THROUGHOUT THE HOUSE...
THE FREQUENTLY EMPTY FRIDGE...
WITH THE OCCASIONAL GRUNTED EXCHANGE ON THE LANDING...
IN AGAIN TONIGHT LOVE?
MMFFH.

TATTOO

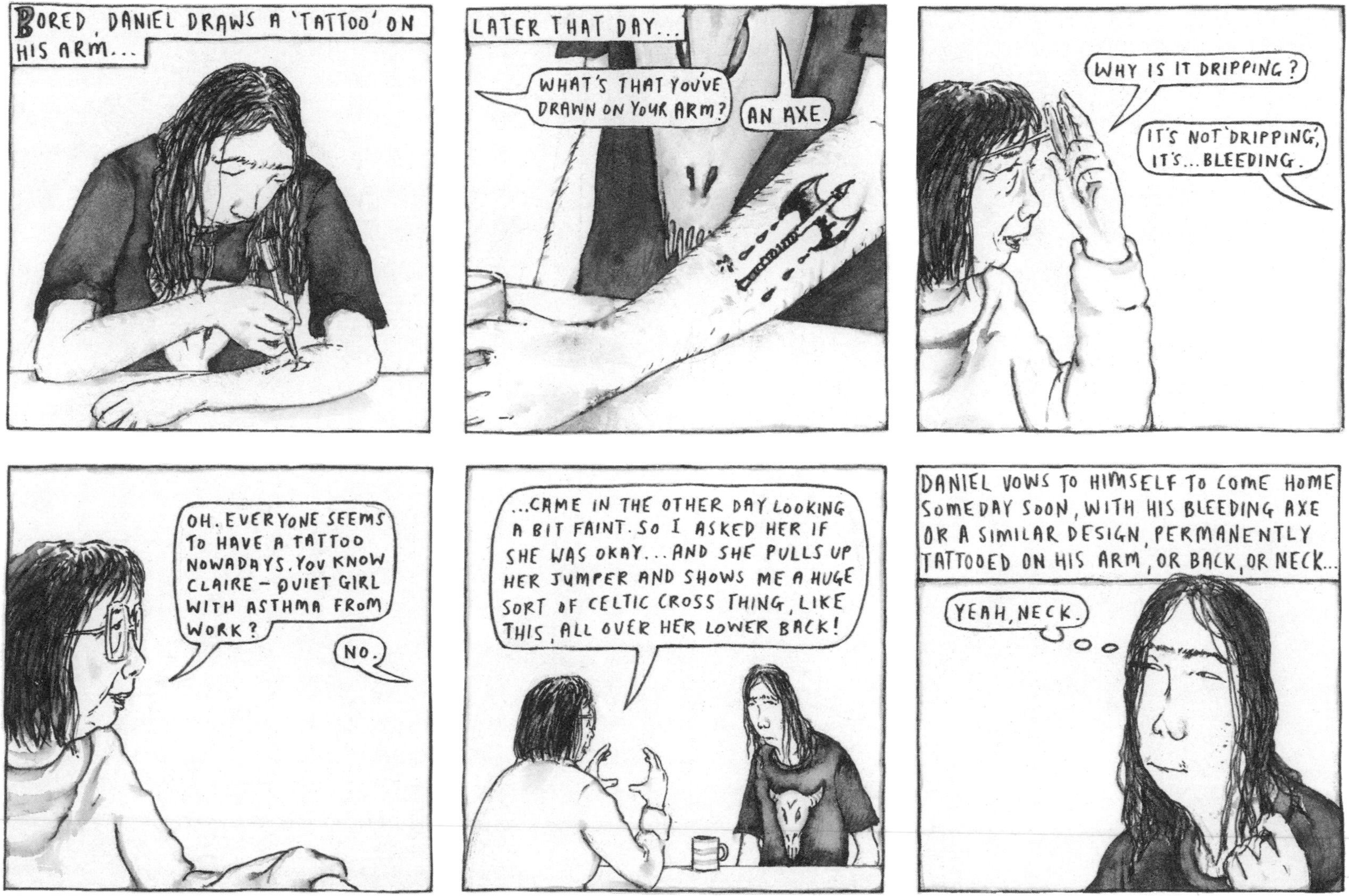
BORED, DANIEL DRAWS A 'TATTOO' ON HIS ARM...
LATER THAT DAY...
WHAT'S THAT YOU'VE DRAWN ON YOUR ARM?
AN AXE.
WHY IS IT DRIPPING?
IT'S NOT 'DRIPPING', IT'S... BLEEDING.
OH. EVERYONE SEEMS TO HAVE A TATTOO NOWADAYS. YOU KNOW CLAIRE - QUIET GIRL WITH ASTHMA FROM WORK?
NO.
...CAME IN THE OTHER DAY LOOKING A BIT FAINT. SO I ASKED HER IF SHE WAS OKAY... AND SHE PULLS UP HER JUMPER AND SHOWS ME A HUGE SORT OF CELTIC CROSS THING, LIKE THIS, ALL OVER HER LOWER BACK!
DANIEL VOWS TO HIMSELF TO COME HOME SOMEDAY SOON, WITH HIS BLEEDING AXE OR A SIMILAR DESIGN, PERMANENTLY TATTOOED ON HIS ARM, OR BACK, OR NECK...
YEAH, NECK.

SHOPPING

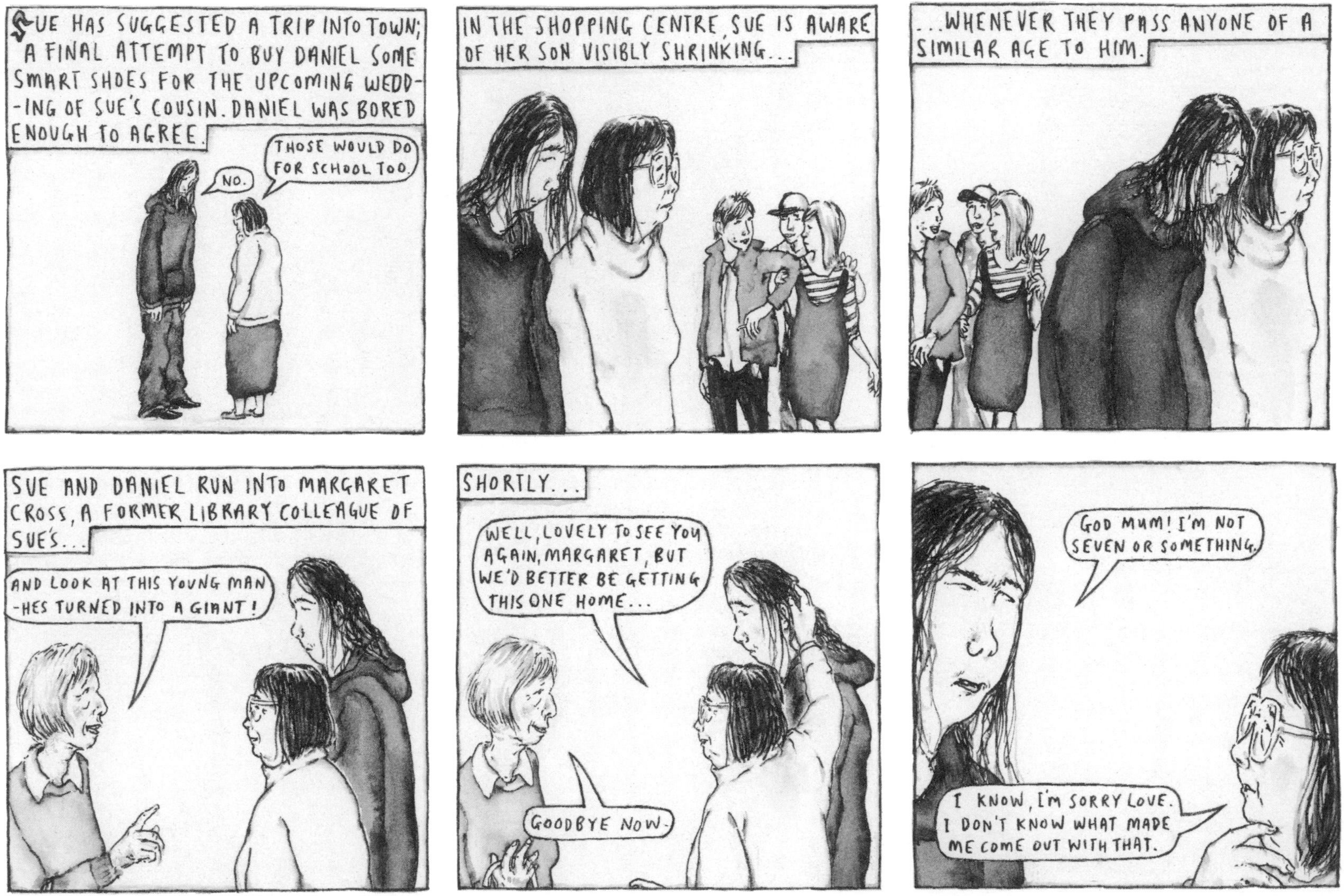
SUE HAS SUGGESTED A TRIP INTO TOWN; A FINAL ATTEMPT TO BUY DANIEL SOME SMART SHOES FOR THE UPCOMING WEDD-ING OF SUE'S COUSIN. DANIEL WAS BORED ENOUGH TO AGREE.
THOSE WOULD DO FOR SCHOOL TOO.
NO.
IN THE SHOPPING CENTRE, SUE IS AWARE OF HER SON VISIBLY SHRINKING...
...WHENEVER THEY PASS ANYONE OF A SIMILAR AGE TO HIM.
SUE AND DANIEL RUN INTO MARGARET CROSS, A FORMER LIBRARY COLLEAGUE OF SUE'S...
AND LOOK AT THIS YOUNG MAN -HES TURNED INTO A GIANT!
SHORTLY...
WELL, LOVELY TO SEE YOU AGAIN, MARGARET, BUT WE'D BETTER BE GETTING THIS ONE HOME...
GOODBYE NOW.
GOD MUM! I'M NOT SEVEN OR SOMETHING.
I KNOW, I'M SORRY LOVE. I DON'T KNOW WHAT MADE ME COME OUT WITH THAT.

MAKEOVER

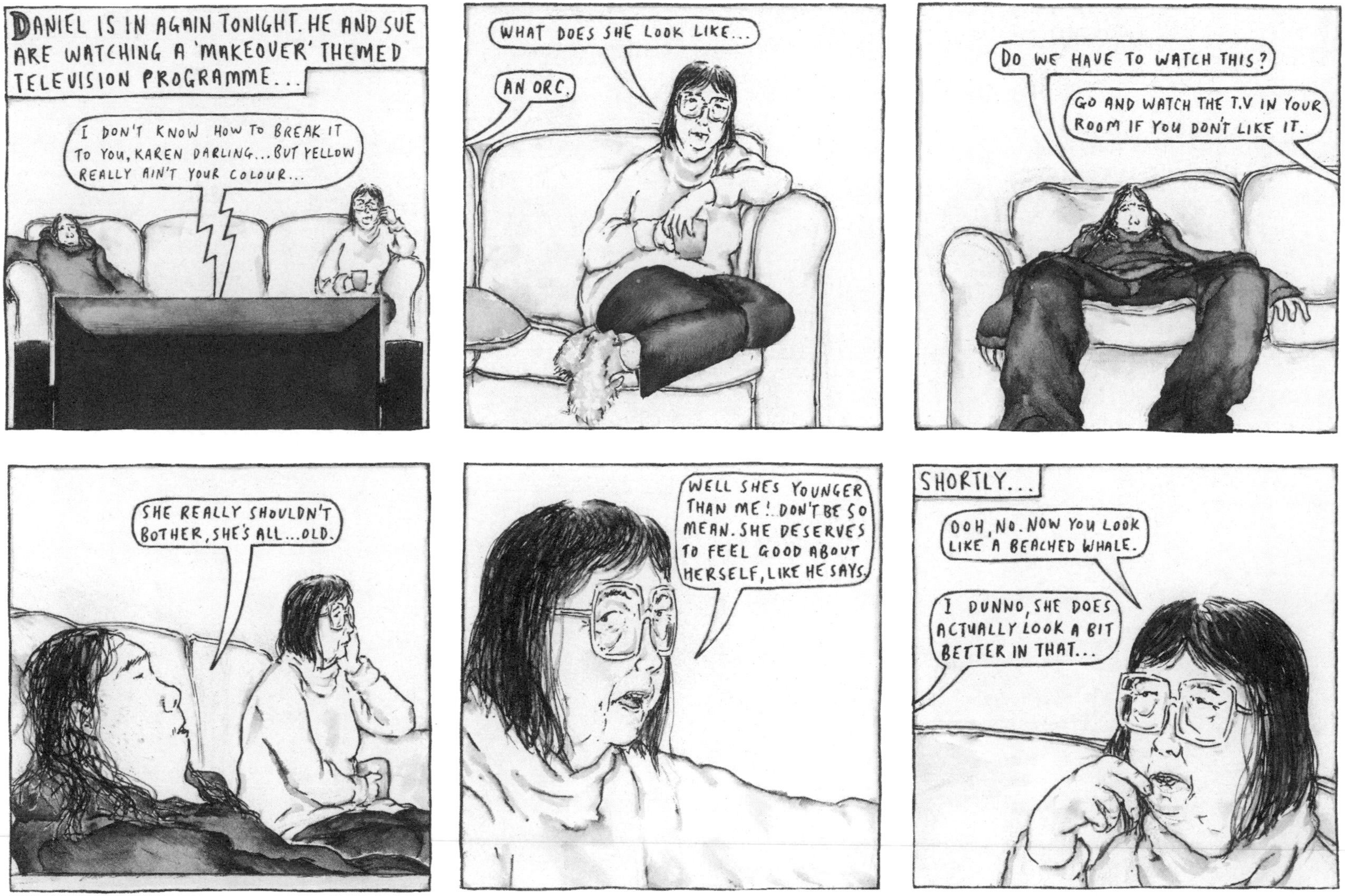
DANIEL IS IN AGAIN TONIGHT. HE AND SUE ARE WATCHING A 'MAKEOVER' THEMED TELEVISION PROGRAMME...
I DON'T KNOW HOW TO BREAK IT TO YOU, KAREN DARLING... BUT YELLOW REALLY AIN'T YOUR COLOUR...
WHAT DOES SHE LOOK LIKE...
AN ORC.
DO WE HAVE TO WATCH THIS?
GO AND WATCH THE T.V IN YOUR ROOM IF YOU DON'T LIKE IT.
SHE REALLY SHOULDN'T BOTHER, SHE'S ALL... OLD.
WELL SHES YOUNGER THAN ME! DON'T BE SO MEAN. SHE DESERVES TO FEEL GOOD ABOUT HERSELF, LIKE HE SAYS.
SHORTLY...
OOH, NO. NOW YOU LOOK LIKE A BEACHED WHALE.
I DUNNO, SHE DOES ACTUALLY LOOK A BIT BETTER IN THAT...

CHIPS

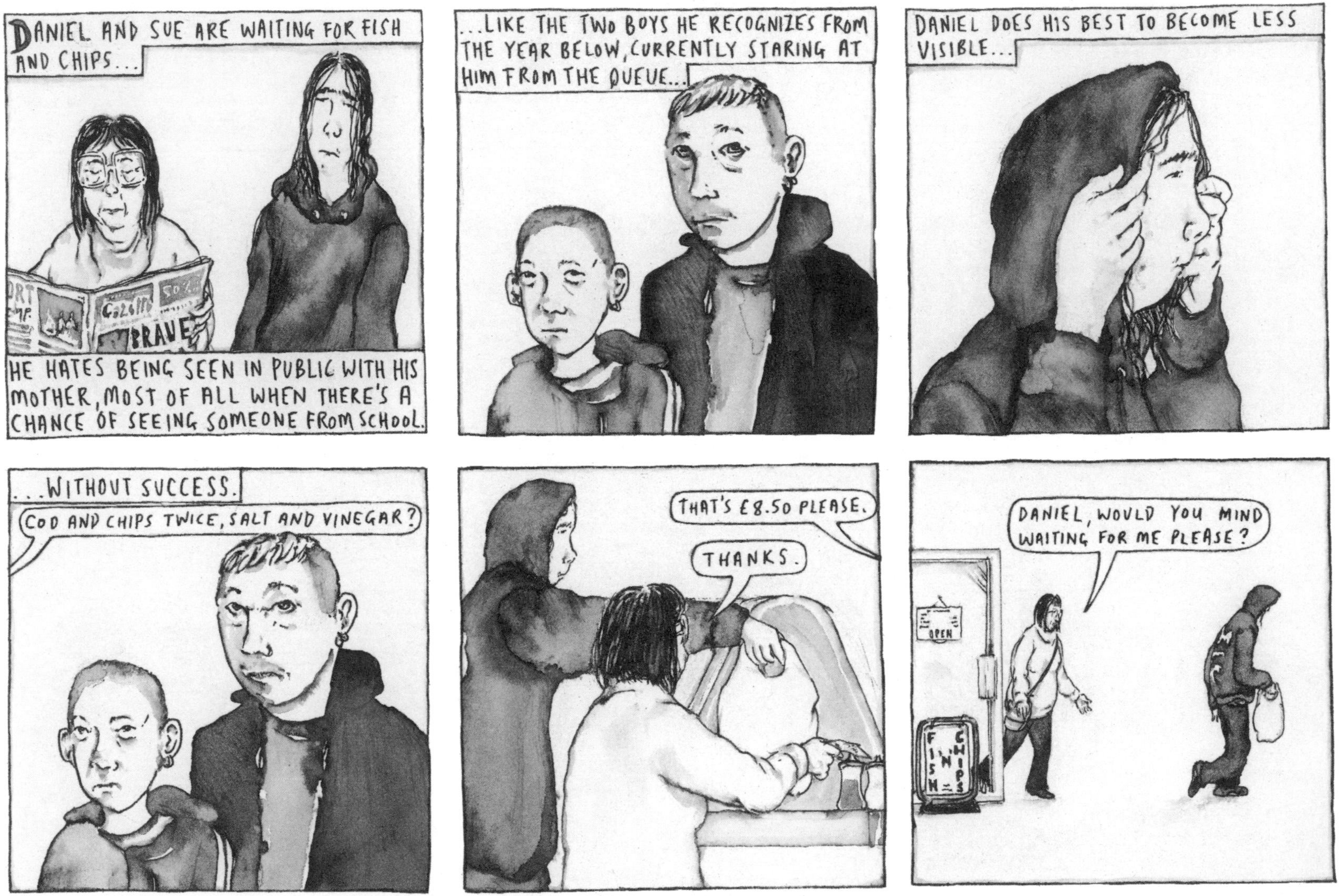
DANIEL AND SUE ARE WAITING FOR FISH AND CHIPS...
HE HATES BEING SEEN IN PUBLIC WITH HIS MOTHER, MOST OF ALL WHEN THERE'S A CHANCE OF SEEING SOMEONE FROM SCHOOL.
...LIKE THE TWO BOYS HE RECOGNIZES FROM THE YEAR BELOW, CURRENTLY STARING AT HIM FROM THE QUEUE...
DANIEL DOES HIS BEST TO BECOME LESS VISIBLE...
...WITHOUT SUCCESS.
COD AND CHIPS TWICE, SALT AND VINEGAR?
THAT'S £8.50 PLEASE.
THANKS.
DANIEL, WOULD YOU MIND WAITING FOR ME PLEASE?
OPEN
FISH N CHIPS

SOFA

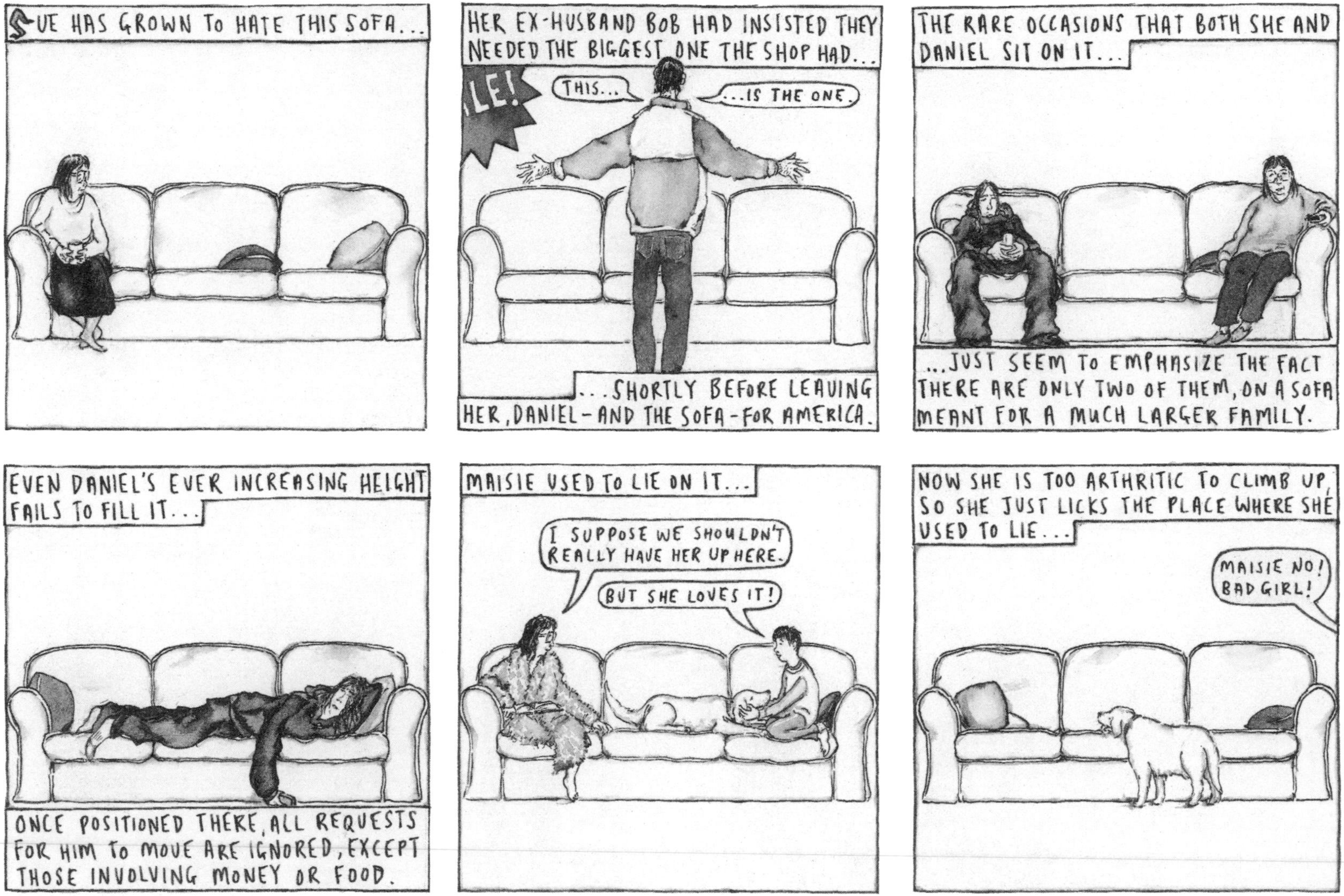
SUE HAS GROWN TO HATE THIS SOFA...
HER EX-HUSBAND BOB HAD INSISTED THEY NEEDED THE BIGGEST ONE THE SHOP HAD...
LE!
THIS...
...IS THE ONE.
...SHORTLY BEFORE LEAVING HER, DANIEL – AND THE SOFA – FOR AMERICA.
THE RARE OCCASIONS THAT BOTH SHE AND DANIEL SIT ON IT...
...JUST SEEM TO EMPHASIZE THE FACT THERE ARE ONLY TWO OF THEM, ON A SOFA MEANT FOR A MUCH LARGER FAMILY.
EVEN DANIEL'S EVER INCREASING HEIGHT FAILS TO FILL IT...
ONCE POSITIONED THERE, ALL REQUESTS FOR HIM TO MOVE ARE IGNORED, EXCEPT THOSE INVOLVING MONEY OR FOOD.
MAISIE USED TO LIE ON IT...
I SUPPOSE WE SHOULDN'T REALLY HAVE HER UP HERE.
BUT SHE LOVES IT!
NOW SHE IS TOO ARTHRITIC TO CLIMB UP, SO SHE JUST LICKS THE PLACE WHERE SHE USED TO LIE...
MAISIE NO! BAD GIRL!

TAXIDERMY

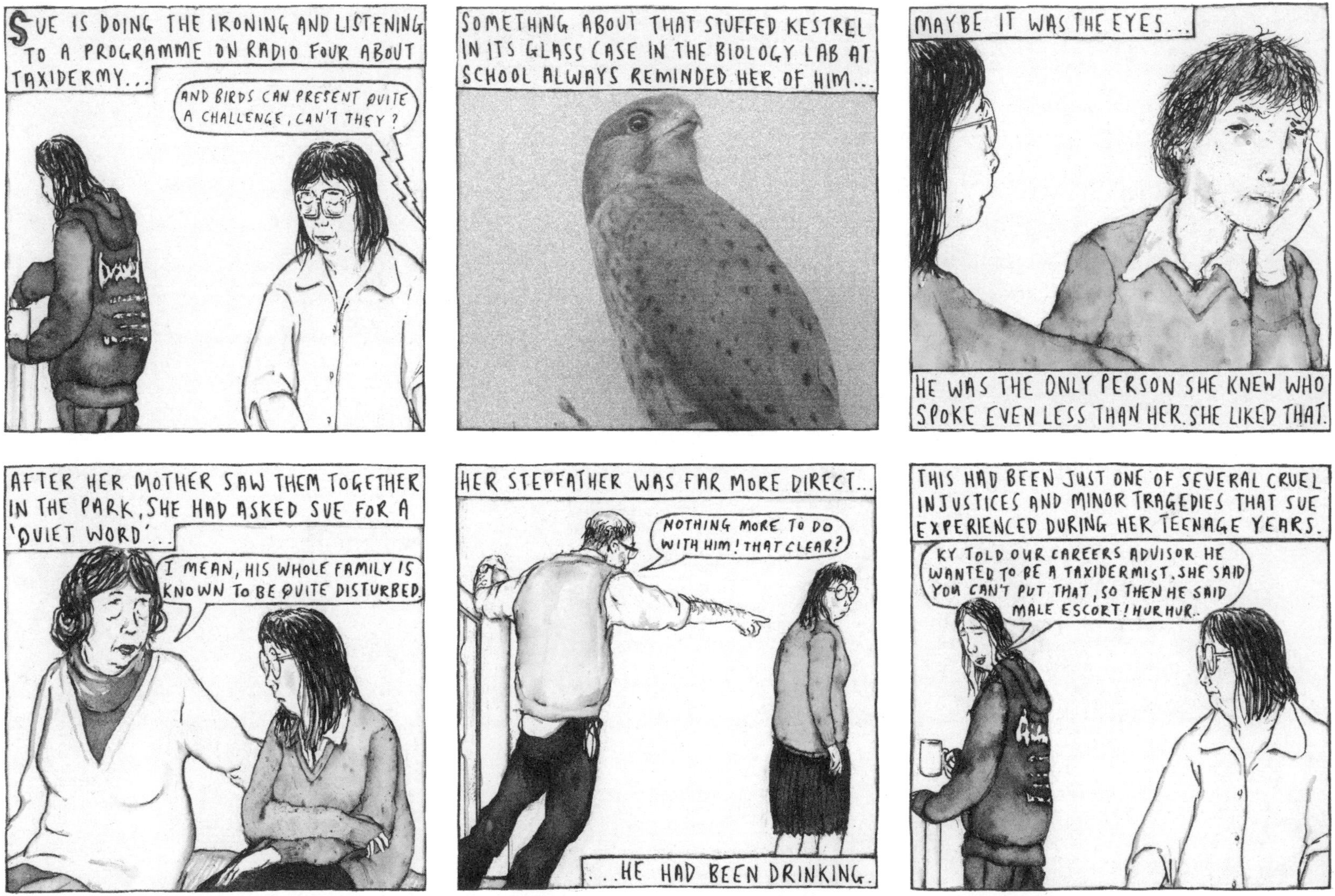
SUE IS DOING THE IRONING AND LISTENING TO A PROGRAMME ON RADIO FOUR ABOUT TAXIDERMY...
AND BIRDS CAN PRESENT QUITE A CHALLENGE, CAN'T THEY?
SOMETHING ABOUT THAT STUFFED KESTREL IN ITS GLASS CASE IN THE BIOLOGY LAB AT SCHOOL ALWAYS REMINDED HER OF HIM...
MAYBE IT WAS THE EYES...
HE WAS THE ONLY PERSON SHE KNEW WHO SPOKE EVEN LESS THAN HER. SHE LIKED THAT.
AFTER HER MOTHER SAW THEM TOGETHER IN THE PARK, SHE HAD ASKED SUE FOR A 'QUIET WORD'...
I MEAN, HIS WHOLE FAMILY IS KNOWN TO BE QUITE DISTURBED.
HER STEPFATHER WAS FAR MORE DIRECT...
NOTHING MORE TO DO WITH HIM! THAT CLEAR?
...HE HAD BEEN DRINKING.
THIS HAD BEEN JUST ONE OF SEVERAL CRUEL INJUSTICES AND MINOR TRAGEDIES THAT SUE EXPERIENCED DURING HER TEENAGE YEARS.
KY TOLD OUR CAREERS ADVISOR HE WANTED TO BE A TAXIDERMIST. SHE SAID YOU CAN'T PUT THAT, SO THEN HE SAID MALE ESCORT! HUR HUR..

SOMEONE

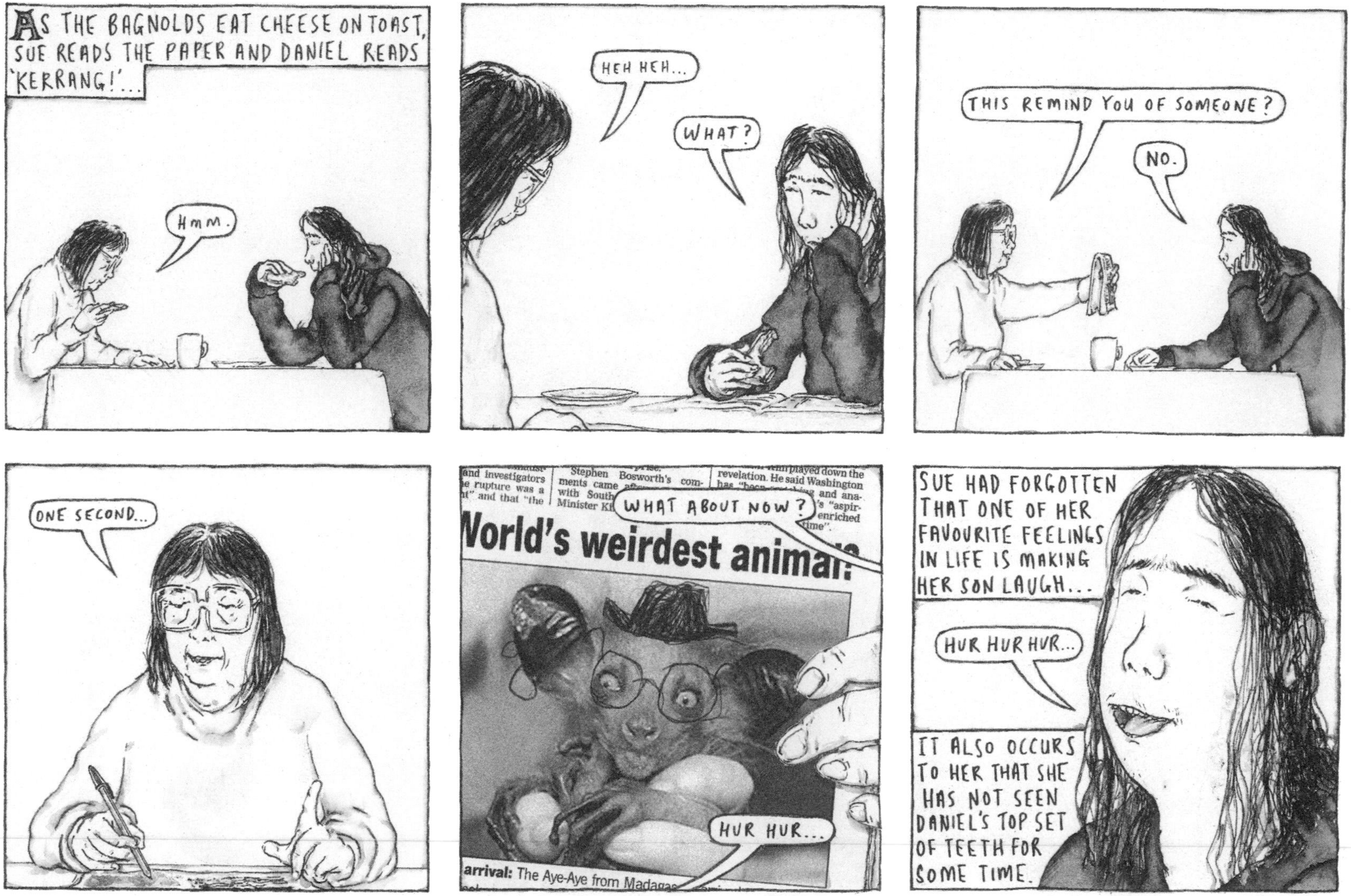
AS THE BAGNOLDS EAT CHEESE ON TOAST, SUE READS THE PAPER AND DANIEL READS 'KERRANG!'...
HMM.
HEH HEH...
WHAT?
THIS REMIND YOU OF SOMEONE?
NO.
ONE SECOND...
WHAT ABOUT NOW?
World's weirdest
HUR HUR...
arrival: The Aye-Aye from
SUE HAD FORGOTTEN THAT ONE OF HER FAVOURITE FEELINGS IN LIFE IS MAKING HER SON LAUGH...
HUR HUR HUR...
IT ALSO OCCURS TO HER THAT SHE HAS NOT SEEN DANIEL'S TOP SET OF TEETH FOR SOME TIME.

STUCK

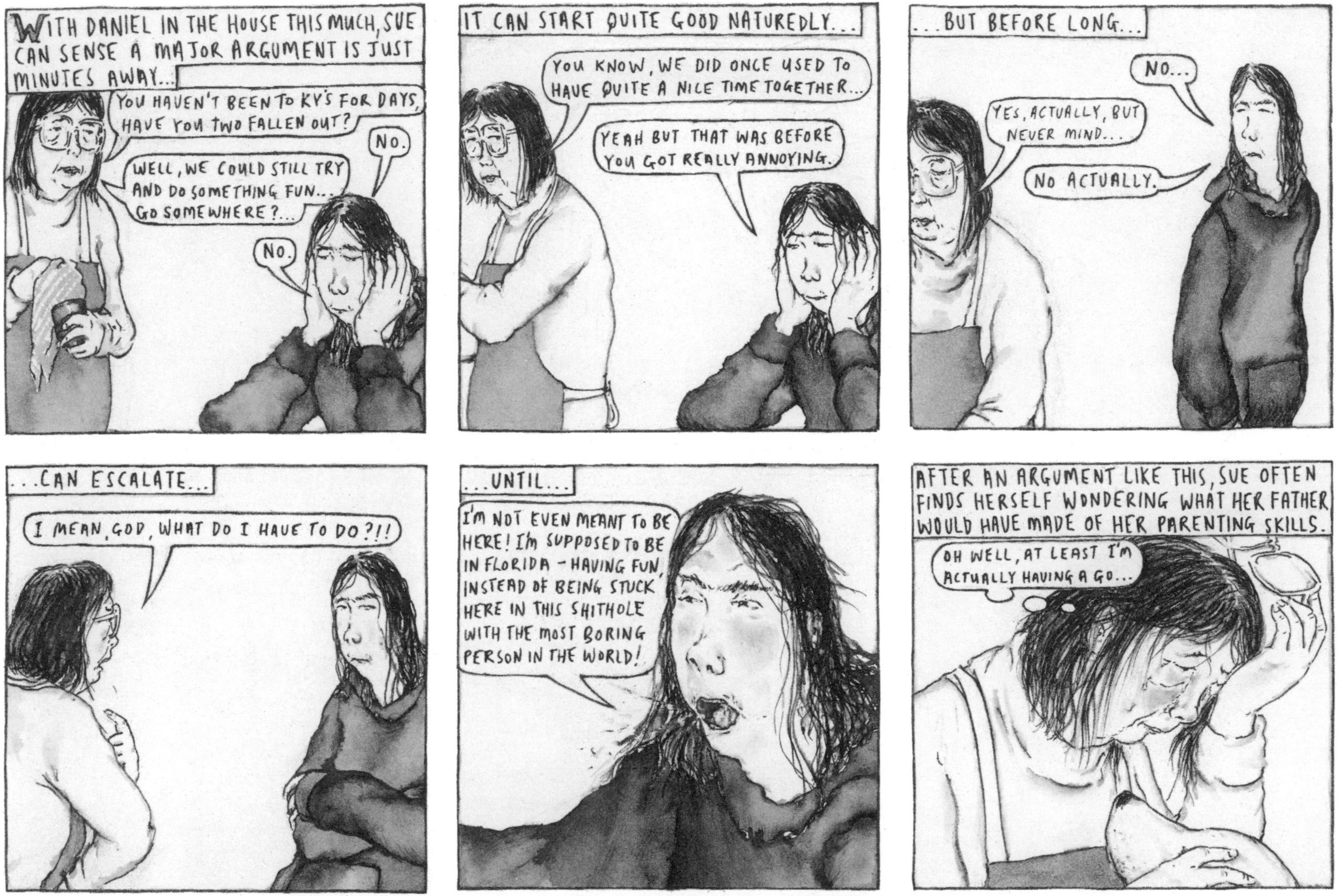
WITH DANIEL IN THE HOUSE THIS MUCH, SUE CAN SENSE A MAJOR ARGUMENT IS JUST MINUTES AWAY...
YOU HAVEN'T BEEN TO KY'S FOR DAYS, HAVE YOU TWO FALLEN OUT?
NO.
WELL, WE COULD STILL TRY AND DO SOMETHING FUN... GO SOMEWHERE?...
NO.
IT CAN START QUITE GOOD NATUREDLY...
YOU KNOW, WE DID ONCE USED TO HAVE QUITE A NICE TIME TOGETHER...
YEAH BUT THAT WAS BEFORE YOU GOT REALLY ANNOYING.
...BUT BEFORE LONG...
NO...
YES, ACTUALLY, BUT NEVER MIND...
NO ACTUALLY.
...CAN ESCALATE...
I MEAN, GOD, WHAT DO I HAVE TO DO?!!
...UNTIL...
I'M NOT EVEN MEANT TO BE HERE! I'M SUPPOSED TO BE IN FLORIDA - HAVING FUN, INSTEAD OF BEING STUCK HERE IN THIS SHITHOLE WITH THE MOST BORING PERSON IN THE WORLD!
AFTER AN ARGUMENT LIKE THIS, SUE OFTEN FINDS HERSELF WONDERING WHAT HER FATHER WOULD HAVE MADE OF HER PARENTING SKILLS.
OH WELL, AT LEAST I'M ACTUALLY HAVING A GO...

HOURS

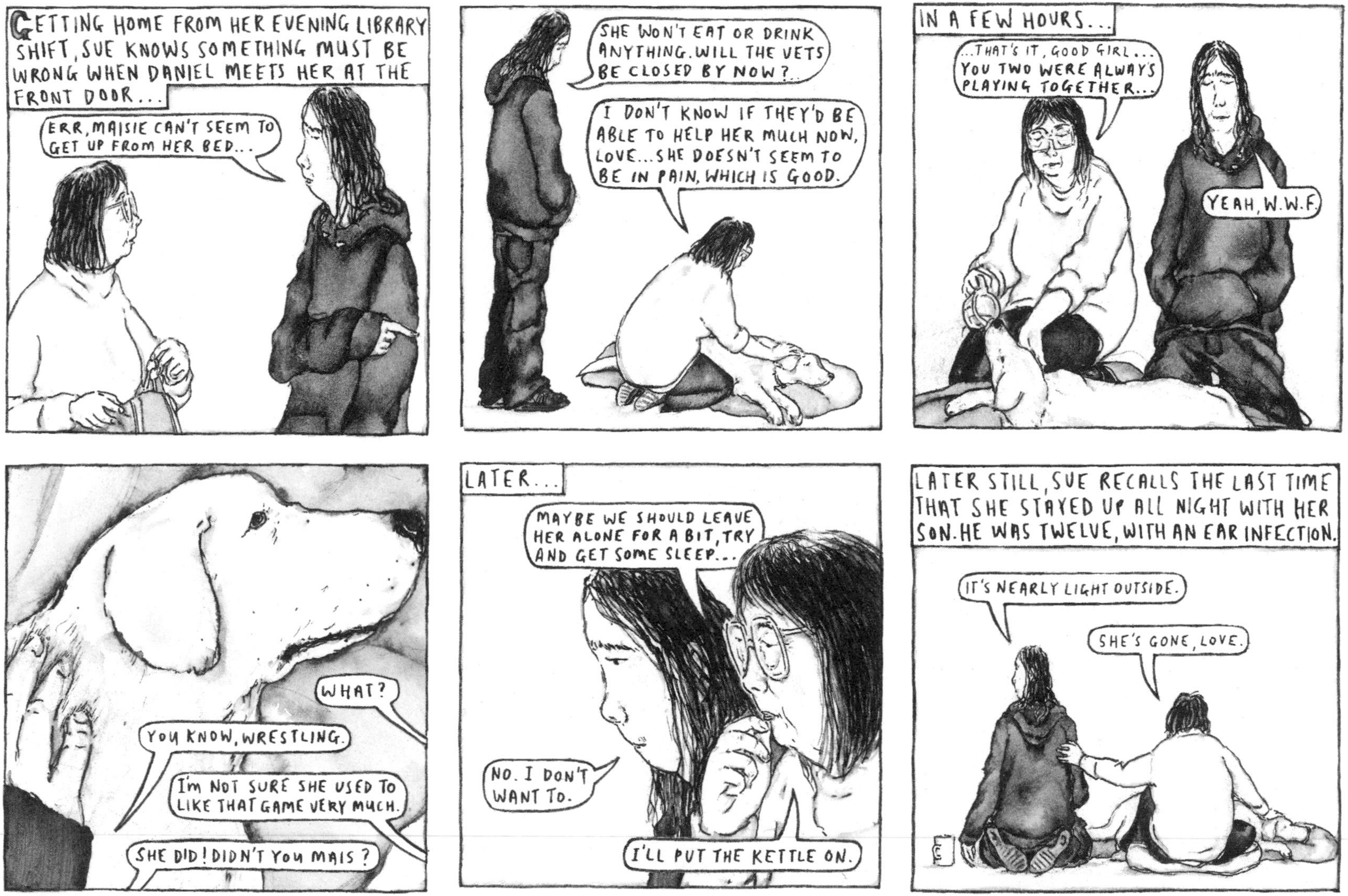
GETTING HOME FROM HER EVENING LIBRARY SHIFT, SUE KNOWS SOMETHING MUST BE WRONG WHEN DANIEL MEETS HER AT THE FRONT DOOR...
ERR, MAISIE CAN'T SEEM TO GET UP FROM HER BED...
SHE WON'T EAT OR DRINK ANYTHING. WILL THE VETS BE CLOSED BY NOW?...
I DON'T KNOW IF THEY'D BE ABLE TO HELP HER MUCH NOW, LOVE... SHE DOESN'T SEEM TO BE IN PAIN, WHICH IS GOOD.
IN A FEW HOURS...
...THAT'S IT, GOOD GIRL... YOU TWO WERE ALWAYS PLAYING TOGETHER...
YEAH, W.W.F.
WHAT?
YOU KNOW, WRESTLING.
I'M NOT SURE SHE USED TO LIKE THAT GAME VERY MUCH.
SHE DID! DIDN'T YOU MAIS?
LATER...
MAYBE WE SHOULD LEAVE HER ALONE FOR A BIT, TRY AND GET SOME SLEEP...
NO. I DON'T WANT TO.
I'LL PUT THE KETTLE ON.
LATER STILL, SUE RECALLS THE LAST TIME THAT SHE STAYED UP ALL NIGHT WITH HER SON. HE WAS TWELVE, WITH AN EAR INFECTION.
IT'S NEARLY LIGHT OUTSIDE.
SHE'S GONE, LOVE.

APART

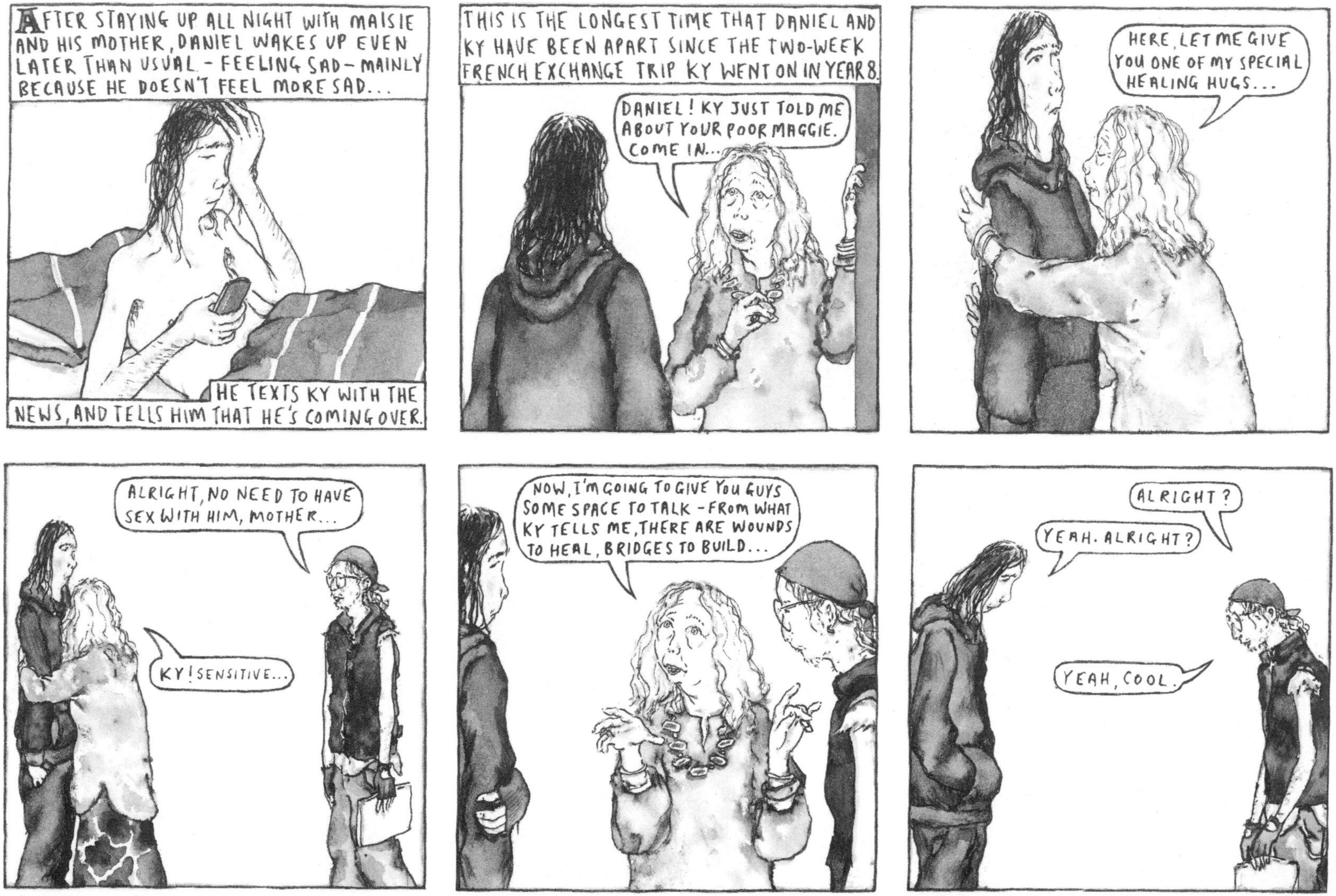
AFTER STAYING UP ALL NIGHT WITH MAISIE AND HIS MOTHER, DANIEL WAKES UP EVEN LATER THAN USUAL - FEELING SAD - MAINLY BECAUSE HE DOESN'T FEEL MORE SAD...
HE TEXTS KY WITH THE NEWS, AND TELLS HIM THAT HE'S COMING OVER.
THIS IS THE LONGEST TIME THAT DANIEL AND KY HAVE BEEN APART SINCE THE TWO-WEEK FRENCH EXCHANGE TRIP KY WENT ON IN YEAR 8.
DANIEL! KY JUST TOLD ME ABOUT YOUR POOR MAGGIE. COME IN...
HERE, LET ME GIVE YOU ONE OF MY SPECIAL HEALING HUGS...
ALRIGHT, NO NEED TO HAVE SEX WITH HIM, MOTHER...
KY! SENSITIVE...
NOW, I'M GOING TO GIVE YOU GUYS SOME SPACE TO TALK - FROM WHAT KY TELLS ME, THERE ARE WOUNDS TO HEAL, BRIDGES TO BUILD...
ALRIGHT?
YEAH. ALRIGHT?
YEAH, COOL.

SIXTH WEEK

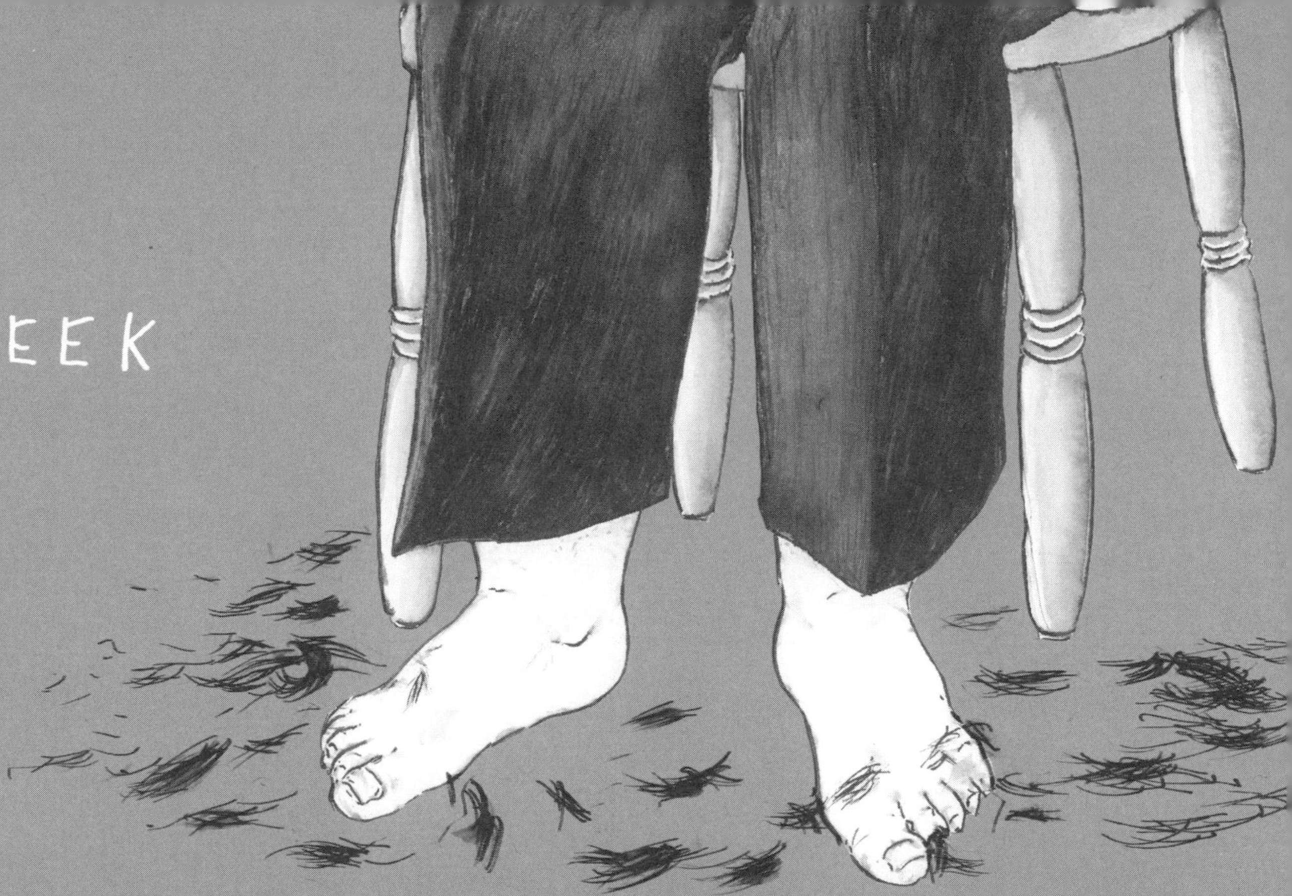

DATE

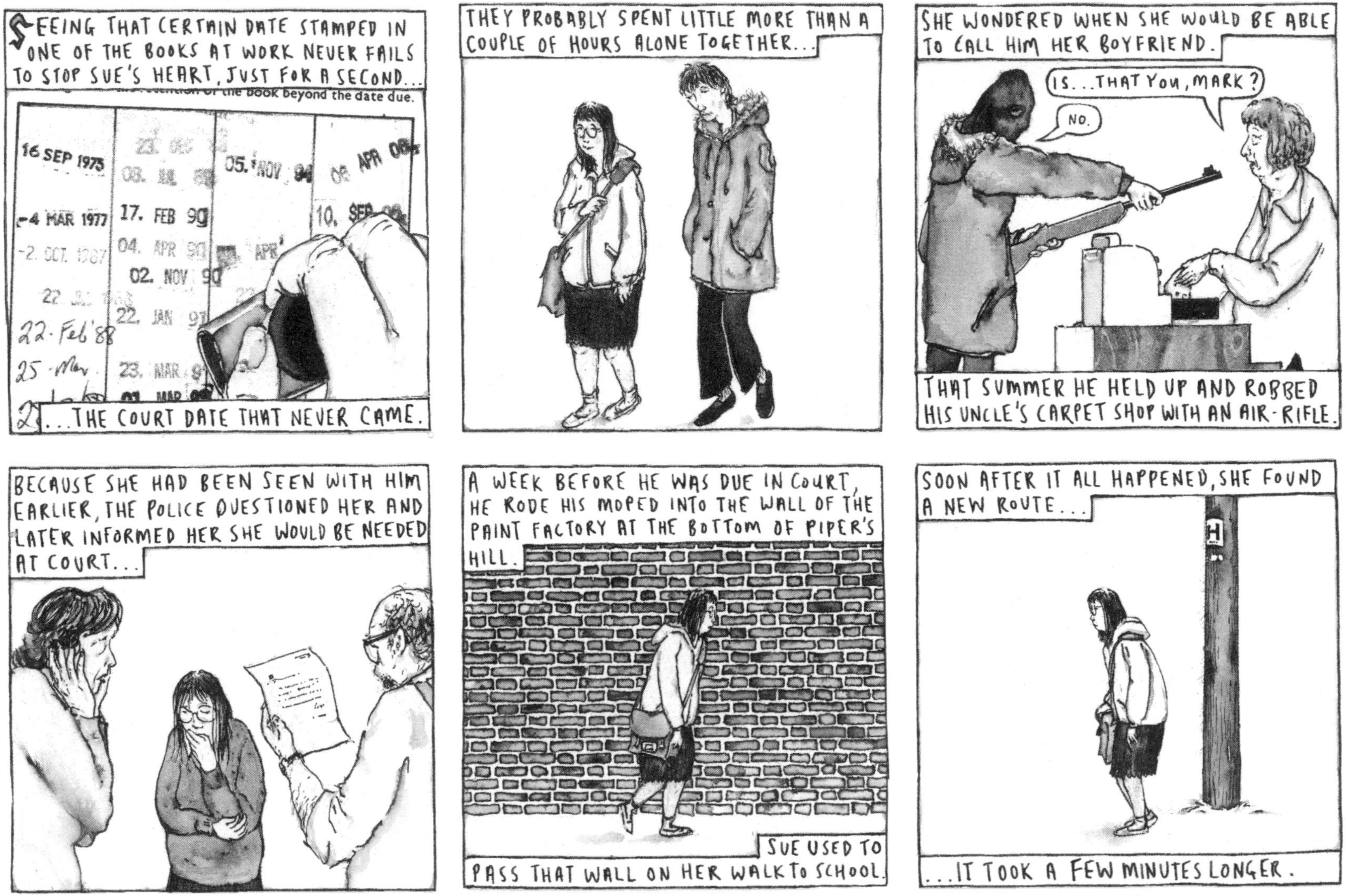
SEEING THAT CERTAIN DATE STAMPED IN ONE OF THE BOOKS AT WORK NEVER FAILS TO STOP SUE'S HEART, JUST FOR A SECOND...
...THE COURT DATE THAT NEVER CAME.
THEY PROBABLY SPENT LITTLE MORE THAN A COUPLE OF HOURS ALONE TOGETHER...
SHE WONDERED WHEN SHE WOULD BE ABLE TO CALL HIM HER BOYFRIEND.
IS...THAT YOU, MARK?
NO.
THAT SUMMER HE HELD UP AND ROBBED HIS UNCLE'S CARPET SHOP WITH AN AIR-RIFLE.
BECAUSE SHE HAD BEEN SEEN WITH HIM EARLIER, THE POLICE QUESTIONED HER AND LATER INFORMED HER SHE WOULD BE NEEDED AT COURT...
A WEEK BEFORE HE WAS DUE IN COURT, HE RODE HIS MOPED INTO THE WALL OF THE PAINT FACTORY AT THE BOTTOM OF PIPER'S HILL.
SUE USED TO PASS THAT WALL ON HER WALK TO SCHOOL.
SOON AFTER IT ALL HAPPENED, SHE FOUND A NEW ROUTE...
...IT TOOK A FEW MINUTES LONGER.

HARD

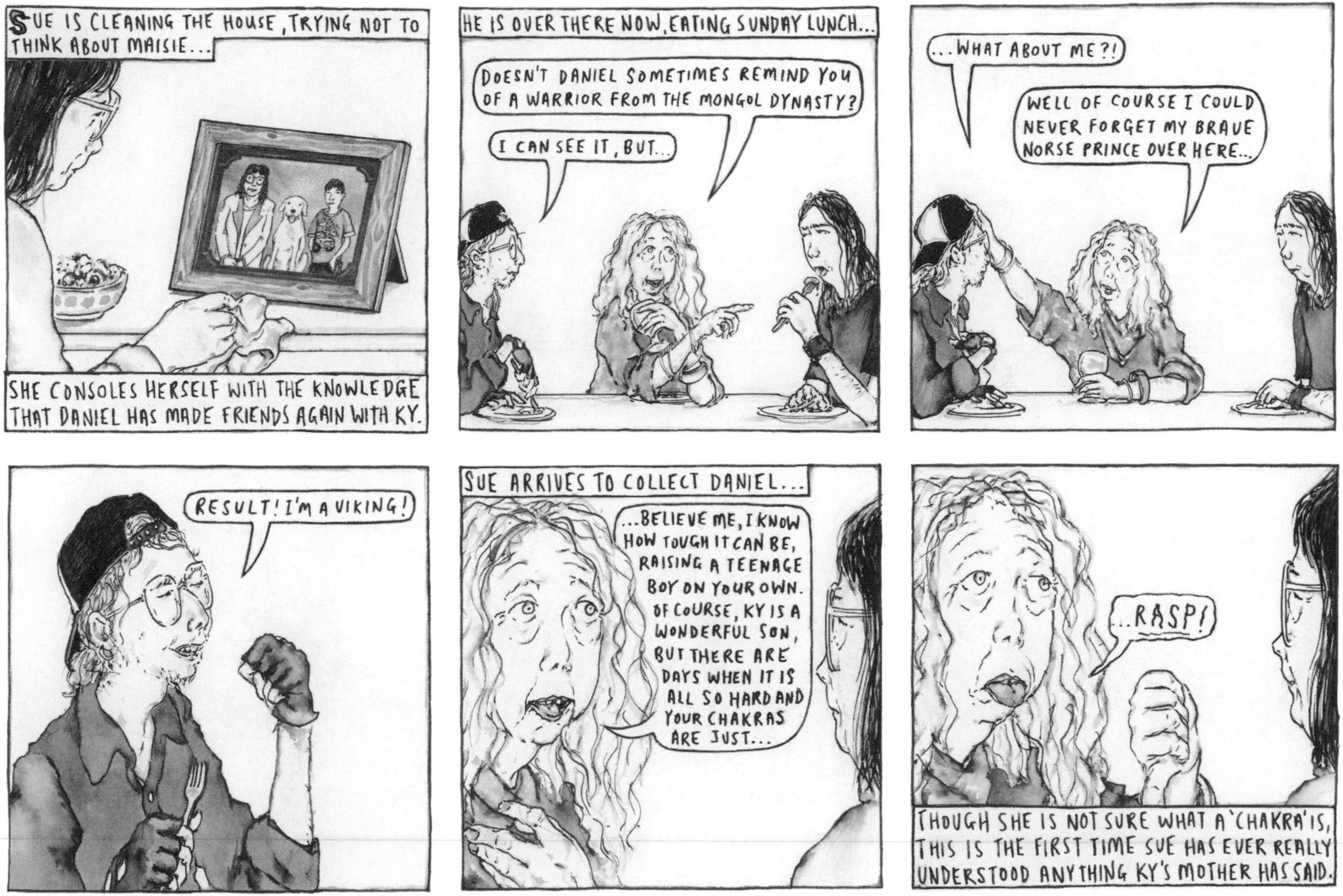
SUE IS CLEANING THE HOUSE, TRYING NOT TO THINK ABOUT MAISIE...
SHE CONSOLES HERSELF WITH THE KNOWLEDGE THAT DANIEL HAS MADE FRIENDS AGAIN WITH KY.
HE IS OVER THERE NOW, EATING SUNDAY LUNCH...
DOESN'T DANIEL SOMETIMES REMIND YOU OF A WARRIOR FROM THE MONGOL DYNASTY?
I CAN SEE IT, BUT...
...WHAT ABOUT ME?!
WELL OF COURSE I COULD NEVER FORGET MY BRAVE NORSE PRINCE OVER HERE...
RESULT! I'M A VIKING!
SUE ARRIVES TO COLLECT DANIEL...
...BELIEVE ME, I KNOW HOW TOUGH IT CAN BE, RAISING A TEENAGE BOY ON YOUR OWN. OF COURSE, KY IS A WONDERFUL SON, BUT THERE ARE DAYS WHEN IT IS ALL SO HARD AND YOUR CHAKRAS ARE JUST...
...RASP!
THOUGH SHE IS NOT SURE WHAT A 'CHAKRA' IS, THIS IS THE FIRST TIME SUE HAS EVER REALLY UNDERSTOOD ANYTHING KY'S MOTHER HAS SAID.

LOOKING

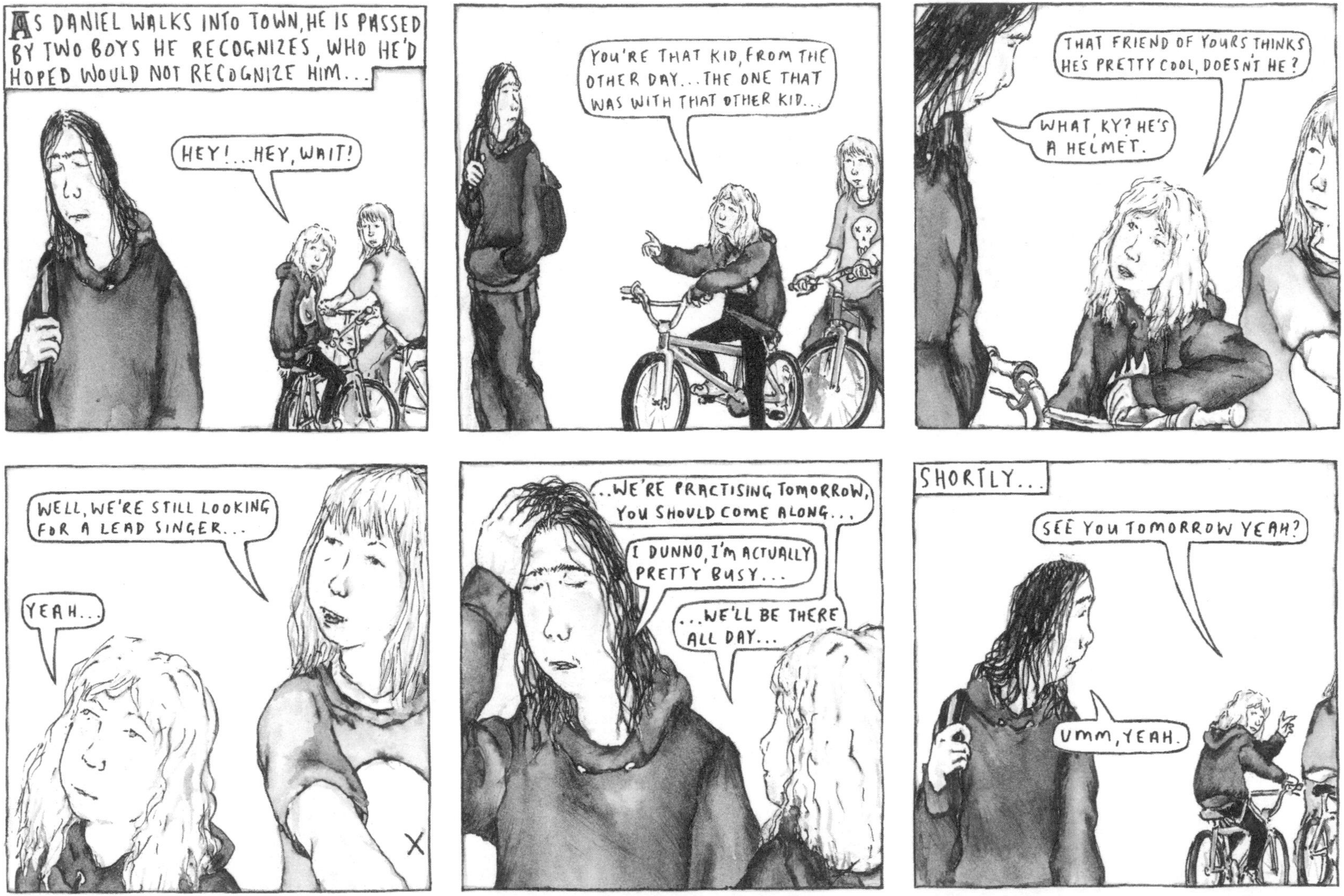
AS DANIEL WALKS INTO TOWN, HE IS PASSED BY TWO BOYS HE RECOGNIZES, WHO HE'D HOPED WOULD NOT RECOGNIZE HIM...
HEY!...HEY, WAIT!
YOU'RE THAT KID, FROM THE OTHER DAY... THE ONE THAT WAS WITH THAT OTHER KID...
THAT FRIEND OF YOURS THINKS HE'S PRETTY COOL, DOESN'T HE?
WHAT, KY? HE'S A HELMET.
WELL, WE'RE STILL LOOKING FOR A LEAD SINGER...
YEAH...
..WE'RE PRACTISING TOMORROW, YOU SHOULD COME ALONG...
I DUNNO, I'M ACTUALLY PRETTY BUSY...
...WE'LL BE THERE ALL DAY...
SHORTLY...
SEE YOU TOMORROW YEAH?
UMM, YEAH.

HAIRCUT

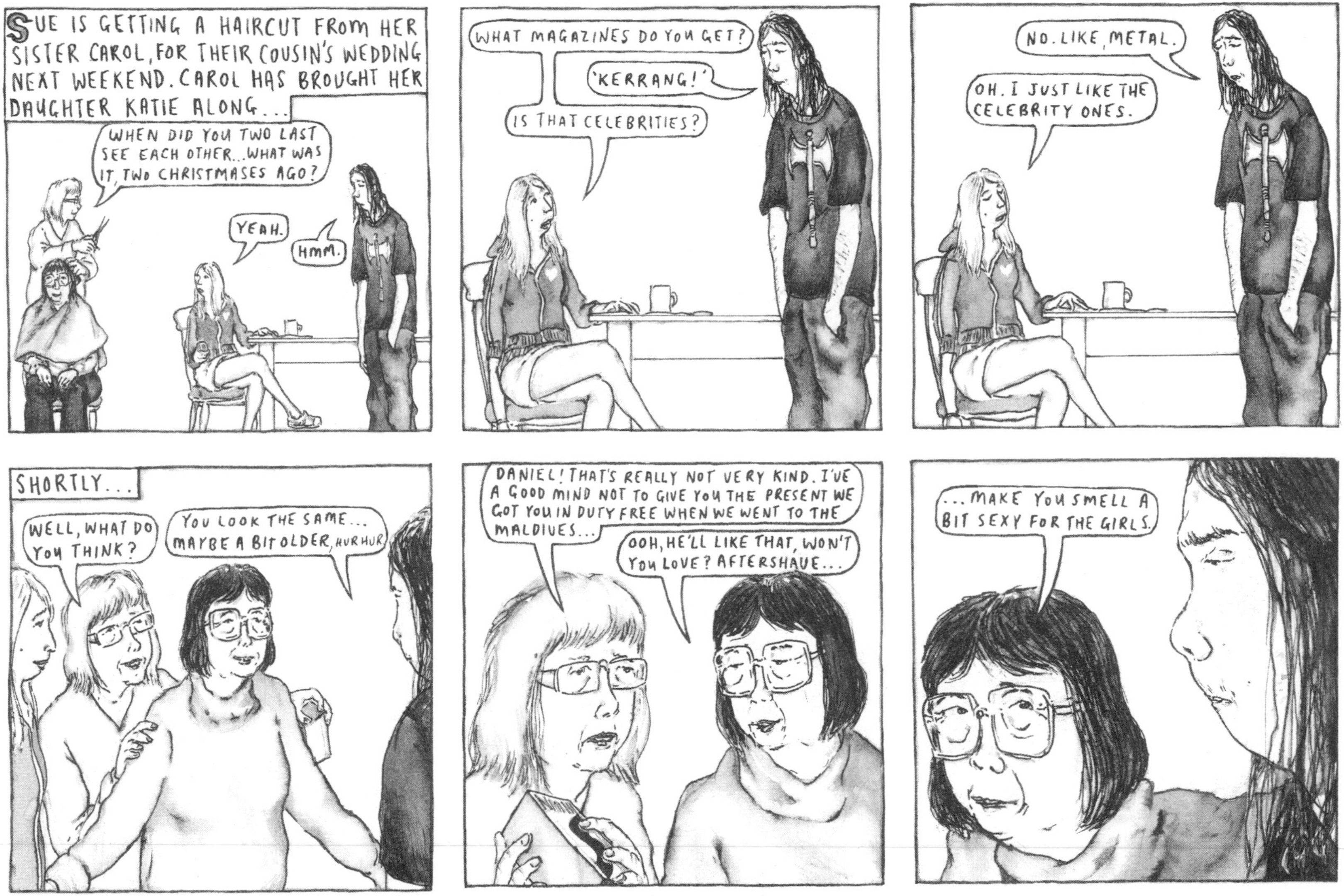
SUE IS GETTING A HAIRCUT FROM HER SISTER CAROL, FOR THEIR COUSIN'S WEDDING NEXT WEEKEND. CAROL HAS BROUGHT HER DAUGHTER KATIE ALONG...
WHEN DID YOU TWO LAST SEE EACH OTHER... WHAT WAS IT, TWO CHRISTMASES AGO?
YEAH.
HMM.
WHAT MAGAZINES DO YOU GET?
'KERRANG!'
IS THAT CELEBRITIES?
NO. LIKE, METAL.
OH. I JUST LIKE THE CELEBRITY ONES.
SHORTLY...
WELL, WHAT DO YOU THINK?
YOU LOOK THE SAME... MAYBE A BIT OLDER, HUR HUR
DANIEL! THAT'S REALLY NOT VERY KIND. I'VE A GOOD MIND NOT TO GIVE YOU THE PRESENT WE GOT YOU IN DUTY FREE WHEN WE WENT TO THE MALDIVES...
OOH, HE'LL LIKE THAT, WON'T YOU LOVE? AFTERSHAVE...
...MAKE YOU SMELL A BIT SEXY FOR THE GIRLS.

SICK

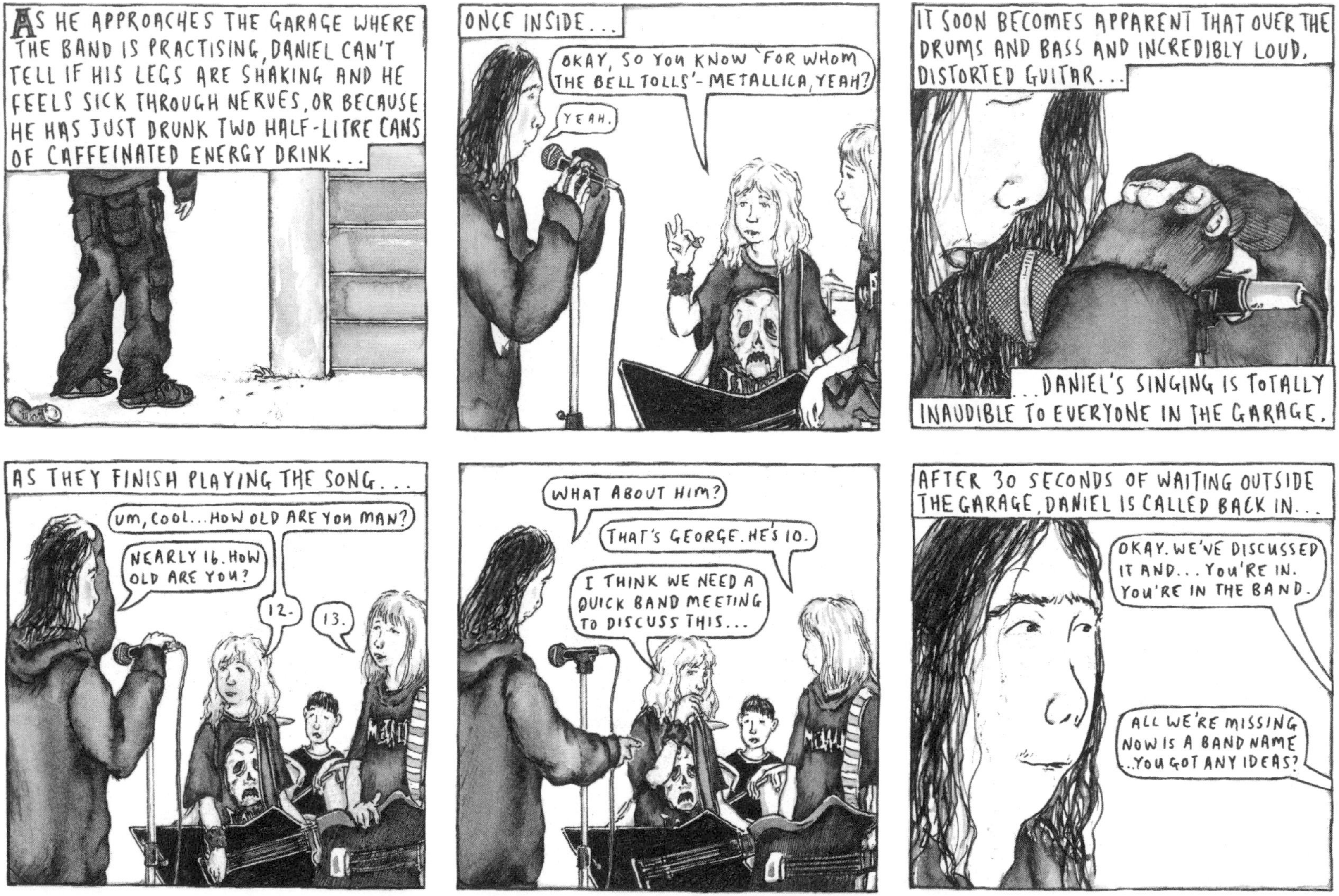

AS HE APPROACHES THE GARAGE WHERE THE BAND IS PRACTISING, DANIEL CAN'T TELL IF HIS LEGS ARE SHAKING AND HE FEELS SICK THROUGH NERVES, OR BECAUSE HE HAS JUST DRUNK TWO HALF-LITRE CANS OF CAFFEINATED ENERGY DRINK...
ONCE INSIDE...
OKAY, SO YOU KNOW 'FOR WHOM THE BELL TOLLS' - METALLICA, YEAH?
YEAH.
IT SOON BECOMES APPARENT THAT OVER THE DRUMS AND BASS AND INCREDIBLY LOUD, DISTORTED GUITAR...
...DANIEL'S SINGING IS TOTALLY INAUDIBLE TO EVERYONE IN THE GARAGE.
AS THEY FINISH PLAYING THE SONG...
UM, COOL... HOW OLD ARE YOU MAN?
NEARLY 16. HOW OLD ARE YOU?
12.
13.
WHAT ABOUT HIM?
THAT'S GEORGE. HE'S 10.
I THINK WE NEED A QUICK BAND MEETING TO DISCUSS THIS...
AFTER 30 SECONDS OF WAITING OUTSIDE THE GARAGE, DANIEL IS CALLED BACK IN...
OKAY. WE'VE DISCUSSED IT AND... YOU'RE IN. YOU'RE IN THE BAND.
ALL WE'RE MISSING NOW IS A BAND NAME ...YOU GOT ANY IDEAS?

MASSAGE

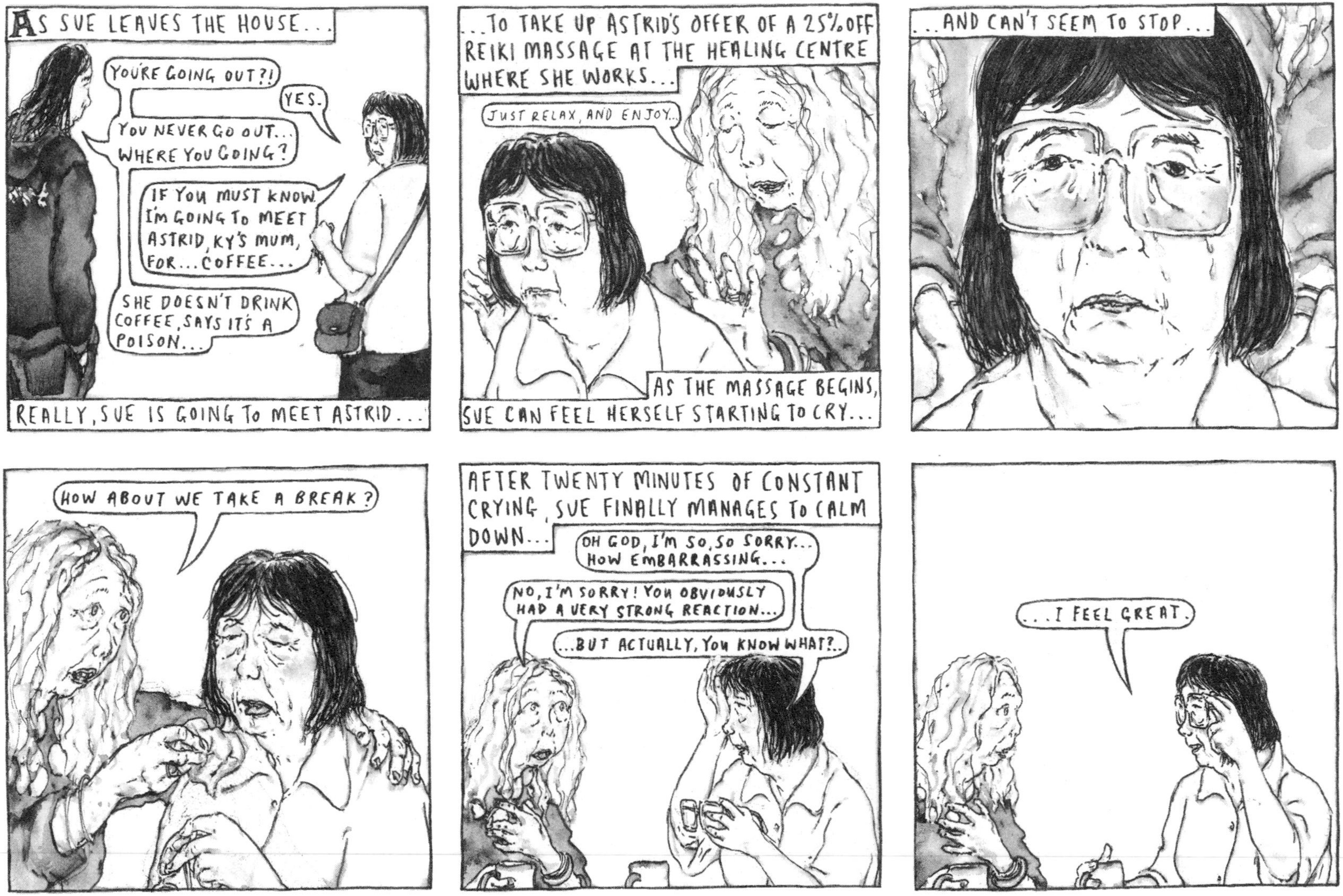

AS SUE LEAVES THE HOUSE...
YOU'RE GOING OUT?!
YES.
YOU NEVER GO OUT... WHERE YOU GOING?
IF YOU MUST KNOW I'M GOING TO MEET ASTRID, KY'S MUM, FOR... COFFEE...
SHE DOESN'T DRINK COFFEE, SAYS IT'S A POISON...
REALLY, SUE IS GOING TO MEET ASTRID...
...TO TAKE UP ASTRID'S OFFER OF A 25% OFF REIKI MASSAGE AT THE HEALING CENTRE WHERE SHE WORKS...
JUST RELAX, AND ENJOY...
AS THE MASSAGE BEGINS, SUE CAN FEEL HERSELF STARTING TO CRY...
...AND CAN'T SEEM TO STOP...
HOW ABOUT WE TAKE A BREAK?
AFTER TWENTY MINUTES OF CONSTANT CRYING, SUE FINALLY MANAGES TO CALM DOWN...
OH GOD, I'M SO, SO SORRY... HOW EMBARRASSING...
NO, I'M SORRY! YOU OBVIOUSLY HAD A VERY STRONG REACTION...
...BUT ACTUALLY, YOU KNOW WHAT?..
...I FEEL GREAT.

WORD

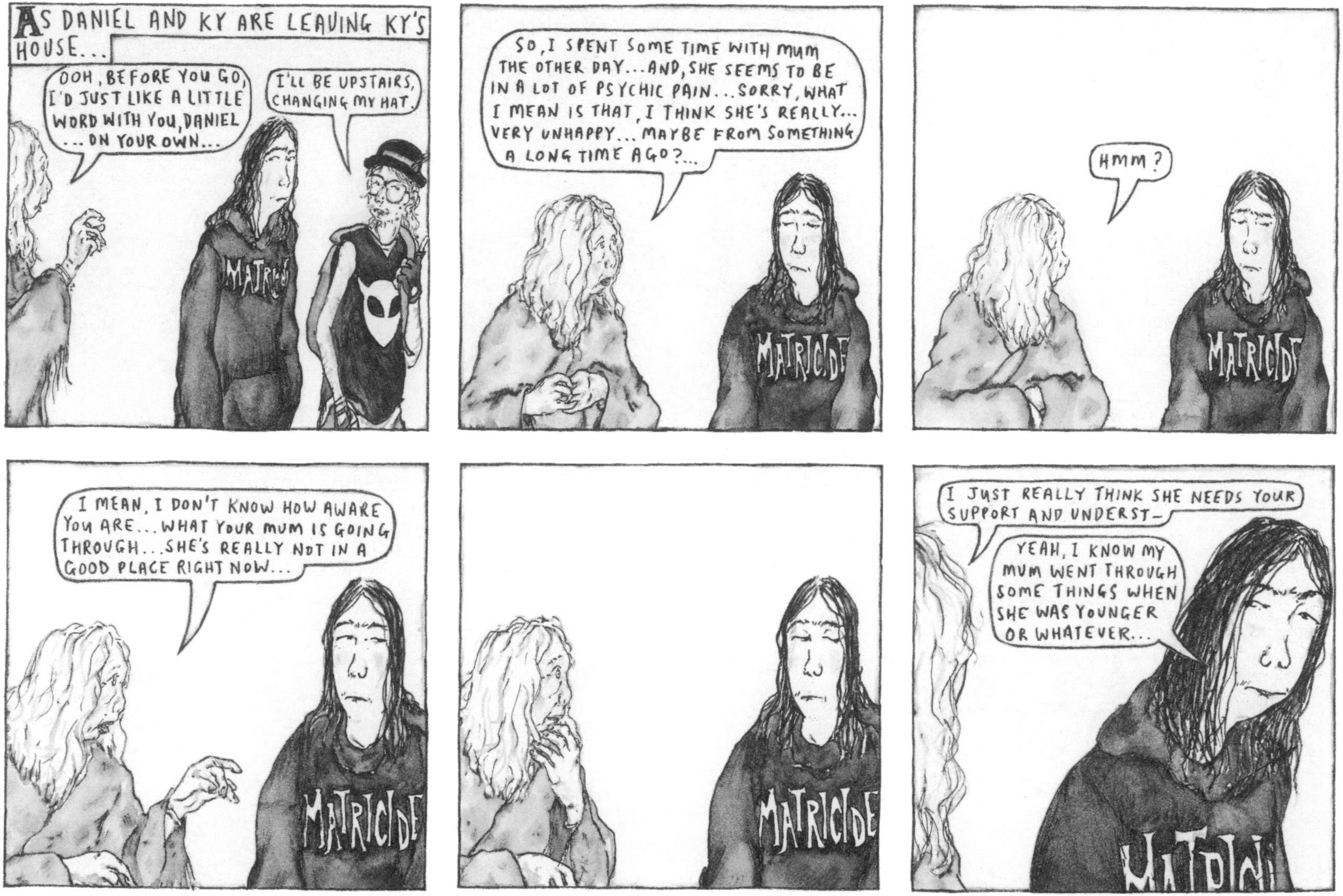
AS DANIEL AND KY ARE LEAVING KY'S HOUSE...
OOH, BEFORE YOU GO, I'D JUST LIKE A LITTLE WORD WITH YOU, DANIEL ...ON YOUR OWN...
I'LL BE UPSTAIRS, CHANGING MY HAT.
MATRICIDE
SO, I SPENT SOME TIME WITH MUM THE OTHER DAY...AND, SHE SEEMS TO BE IN A LOT OF PSYCHIC PAIN...SORRY, WHAT I MEAN IS THAT, I THINK SHE'S REALLY... VERY UNHAPPY... MAYBE FROM SOMETHING A LONG TIME AGO?...
MATRICIDE
HMM?
MATRICIDE
I MEAN, I DON'T KNOW HOW AWARE YOU ARE... WHAT YOUR MUM IS GOING THROUGH...SHE'S REALLY NOT IN A GOOD PLACE RIGHT NOW...
MATRICIDE
MATRICIDE
I JUST REALLY THINK SHE NEEDS YOUR SUPPORT AND UNDERST—
YEAH, I KNOW MY MUM WENT THROUGH SOME THINGS WHEN SHE WAS YOUNGER OR WHATEVER...

STRATEGY

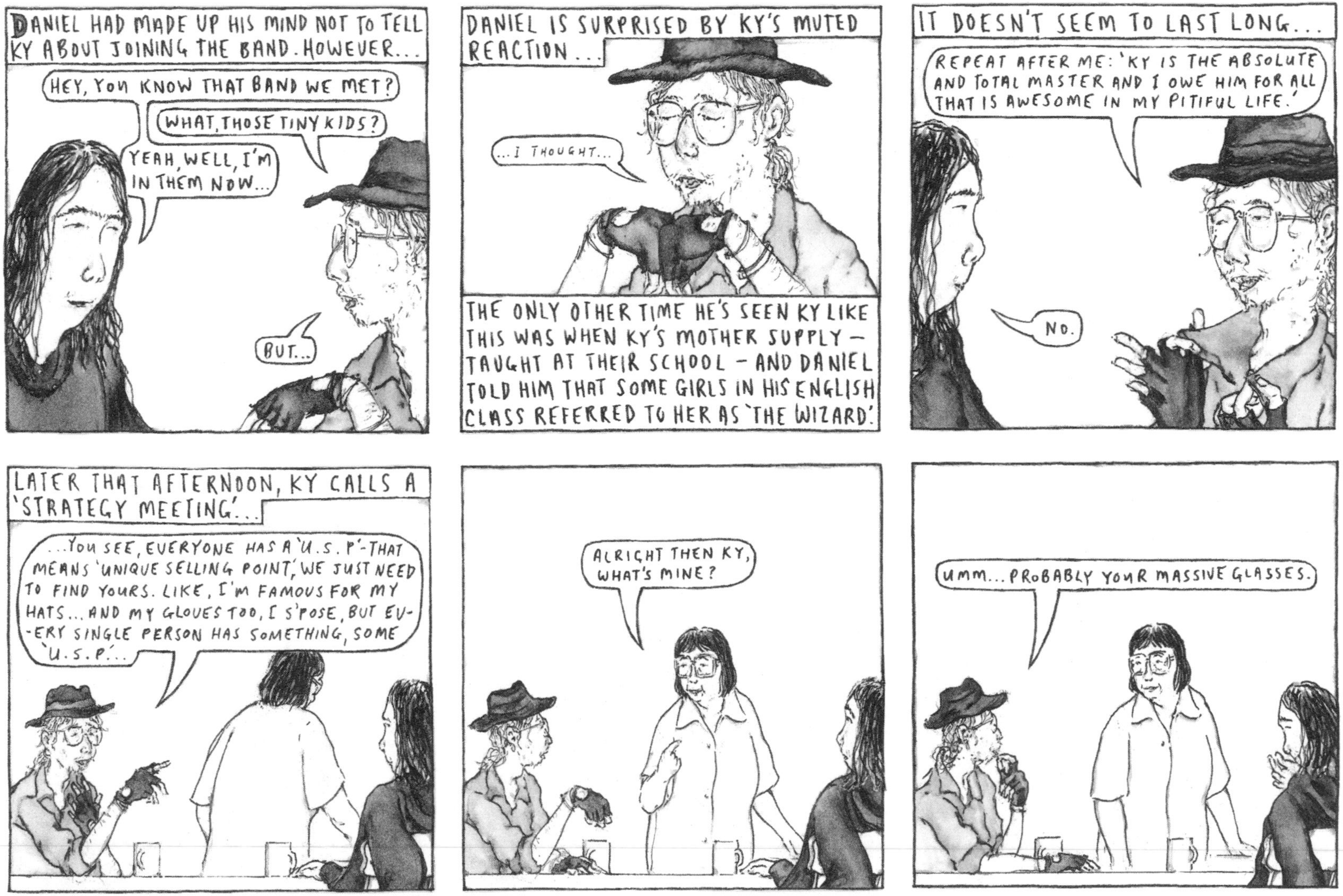
DANIEL HAD MADE UP HIS MIND NOT TO TELL KY ABOUT JOINING THE BAND. HOWEVER...
HEY, YOU KNOW THAT BAND WE MET?
WHAT, THOSE TINY KIDS?
YEAH, WELL, I'M IN THEM NOW...
BUT...
DANIEL IS SURPRISED BY KY'S MUTED REACTION...
...I THOUGHT...
THE ONLY OTHER TIME HE'S SEEN KY LIKE THIS WAS WHEN KY'S MOTHER SUPPLY-TAUGHT AT THEIR SCHOOL - AND DANIEL TOLD HIM THAT SOME GIRLS IN HIS ENGLISH CLASS REFERRED TO HER AS 'THE WIZARD'.
IT DOESN'T SEEM TO LAST LONG...
REPEAT AFTER ME: 'KY IS THE ABSOLUTE AND TOTAL MASTER AND I OWE HIM FOR ALL THAT IS AWESOME IN MY PITIFUL LIFE.'
NO.
LATER THAT AFTERNOON, KY CALLS A 'STRATEGY MEETING'...
...YOU SEE, EVERYONE HAS A 'U.S.P.' - THAT MEANS 'UNIQUE SELLING POINT', WE JUST NEED TO FIND YOURS. LIKE, I'M FAMOUS FOR MY HATS... AND MY GLOVES TOO, I S'POSE, BUT EV-ERY SINGLE PERSON HAS SOMETHING, SOME 'U.S.P.'...
ALRIGHT THEN KY, WHAT'S MINE?
UMM... PROBABLY YOUR MASSIVE GLASSES.

PLAYING

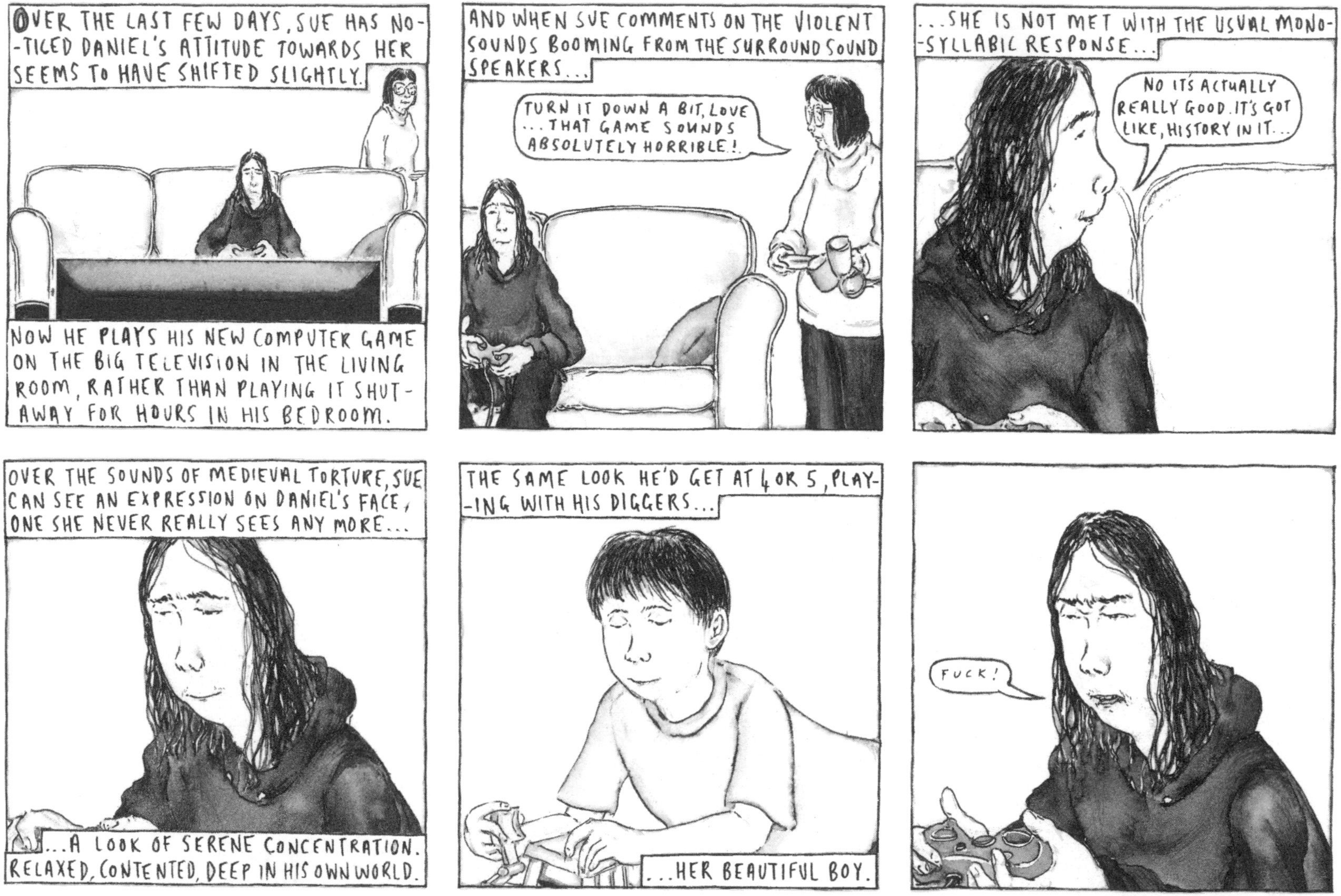
OVER THE LAST FEW DAYS, SUE HAS NO-TICED DANIEL'S ATTITUDE TOWARDS HER SEEMS TO HAVE SHIFTED SLIGHTLY.
NOW HE PLAYS HIS NEW COMPUTER GAME ON THE BIG TELEVISION IN THE LIVING ROOM, RATHER THAN PLAYING IT SHUT-AWAY FOR HOURS IN HIS BEDROOM.
AND WHEN SUE COMMENTS ON THE VIOLENT SOUNDS BOOMING FROM THE SURROUND SOUND SPEAKERS...
TURN IT DOWN A BIT, LOVE ... THAT GAME SOUNDS ABSOLUTELY HORRIBLE!
...SHE IS NOT MET WITH THE USUAL MONO-SYLLABIC RESPONSE...
NO IT'S ACTUALLY REALLY GOOD. IT'S GOT LIKE, HISTORY IN IT...
OVER THE SOUNDS OF MEDIEVAL TORTURE, SUE CAN SEE AN EXPRESSION ON DANIEL'S FACE, ONE SHE NEVER REALLY SEES ANY MORE...
...A LOOK OF SERENE CONCENTRATION. RELAXED, CONTENTED, DEEP IN HIS OWN WORLD.
THE SAME LOOK HE'D GET AT 4 OR 5, PLAY-ING WITH HIS DIGGERS...
...HER BEAUTIFUL BOY.
FUCK!

WEDDING

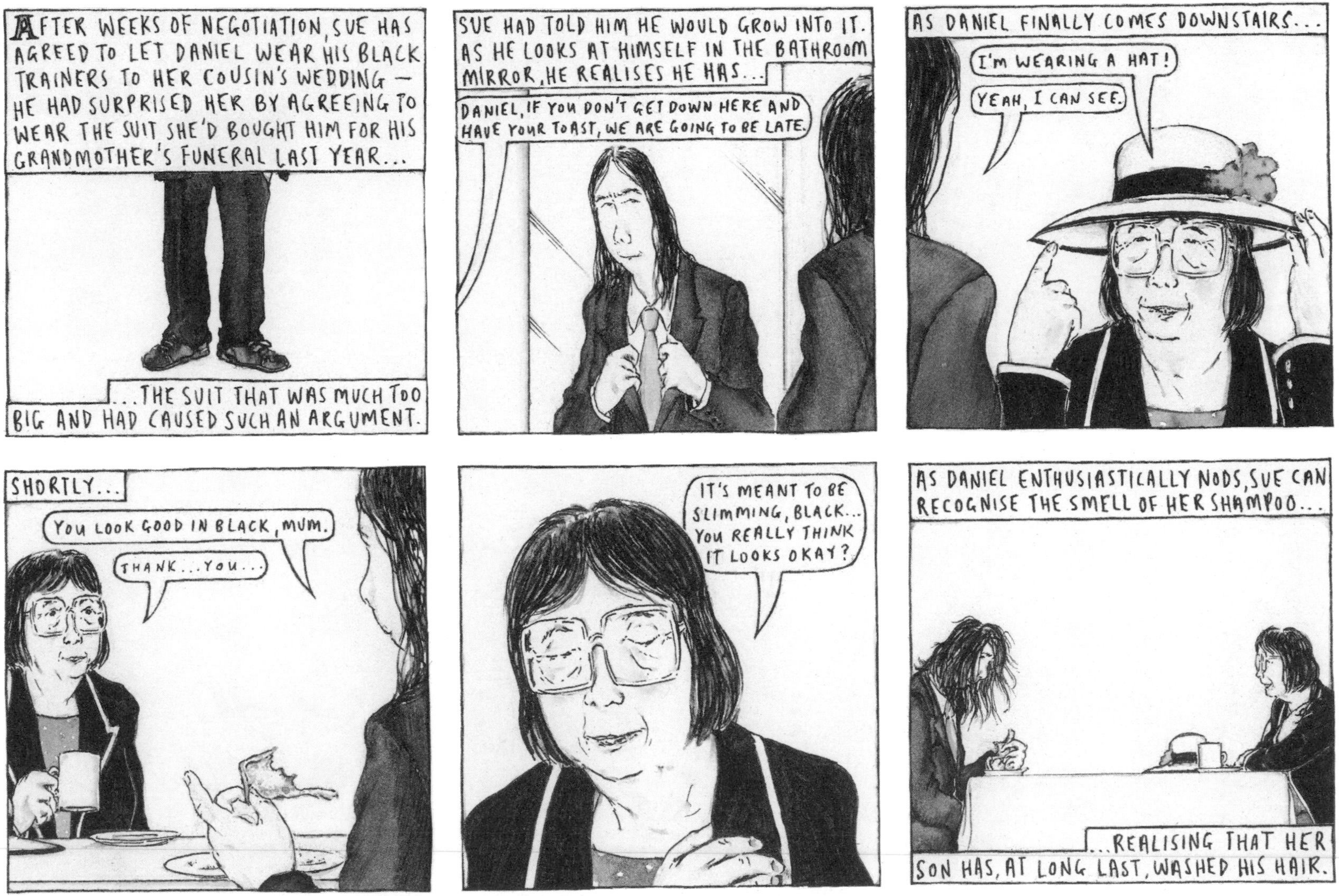
AFTER WEEKS OF NEGOTIATION, SUE HAS AGREED TO LET DANIEL WEAR HIS BLACK TRAINERS TO HER COUSIN'S WEDDING – HE HAD SURPRISED HER BY AGREEING TO WEAR THE SUIT SHE'D BOUGHT HIM FOR HIS GRANDMOTHER'S FUNERAL LAST YEAR...
...THE SUIT THAT WAS MUCH TOO BIG AND HAD CAUSED SUCH AN ARGUMENT.
SUE HAD TOLD HIM HE WOULD GROW INTO IT. AS HE LOOKS AT HIMSELF IN THE BATHROOM MIRROR, HE REALISES HE HAS...
DANIEL, IF YOU DON'T GET DOWN HERE AND HAVE YOUR TOAST, WE ARE GOING TO BE LATE.
AS DANIEL FINALLY COMES DOWNSTAIRS...
I'M WEARING A HAT!
YEAH, I CAN SEE.
SHORTLY...
YOU LOOK GOOD IN BLACK, MUM.
THANK...YOU...
IT'S MEANT TO BE SLIMMING, BLACK... YOU REALLY THINK IT LOOKS OKAY?
AS DANIEL ENTHUSIASTICALLY NODS, SUE CAN RECOGNISE THE SMELL OF HER SHAMPOO...
...REALISING THAT HER SON HAS, AT LONG LAST, WASHED HIS HAIR.

DAYS

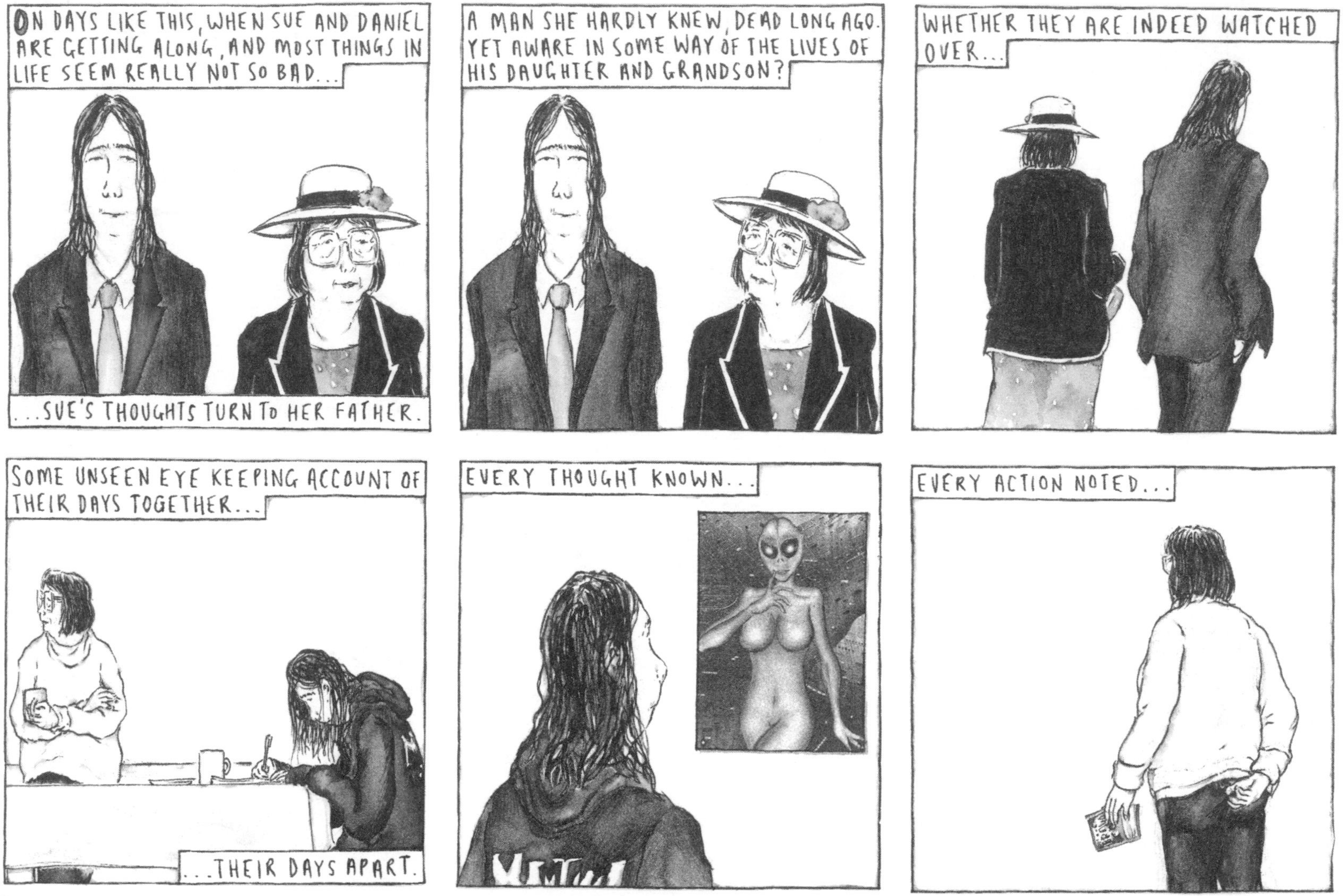
ON DAYS LIKE THIS, WHEN SUE AND DANIEL ARE GETTING ALONG, AND MOST THINGS IN LIFE SEEM REALLY NOT SO BAD...
...SUE'S THOUGHTS TURN TO HER FATHER.
A MAN SHE HARDLY KNEW, DEAD LONG AGO. YET AWARE IN SOME WAY OF THE LIVES OF HIS DAUGHTER AND GRANDSON?
WHETHER THEY ARE INDEED WATCHED OVER...
SOME UNSEEN EYE KEEPING ACCOUNT OF THEIR DAYS TOGETHER...
...THEIR DAYS APART.
EVERY THOUGHT KNOWN...
EVERY ACTION NOTED...

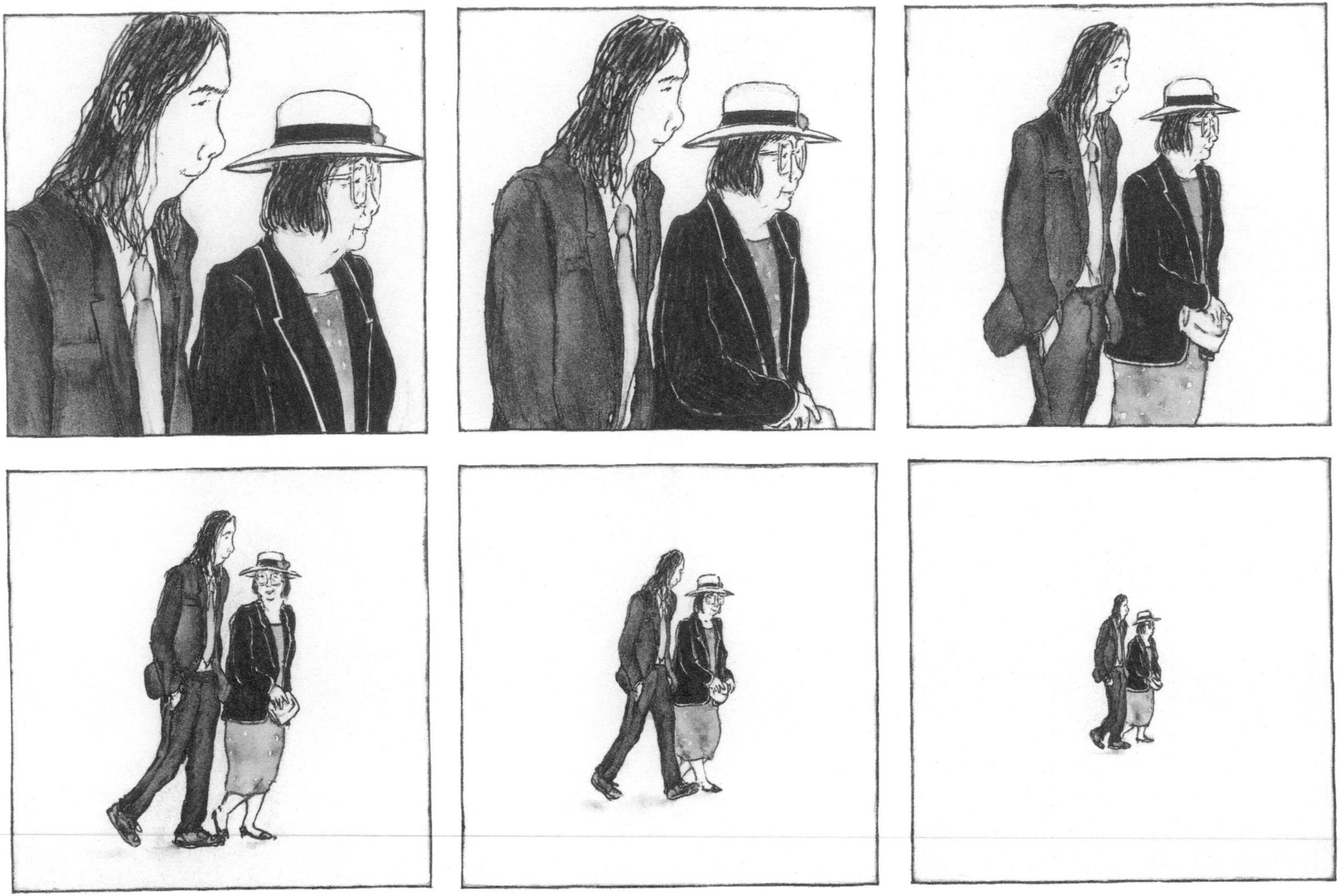

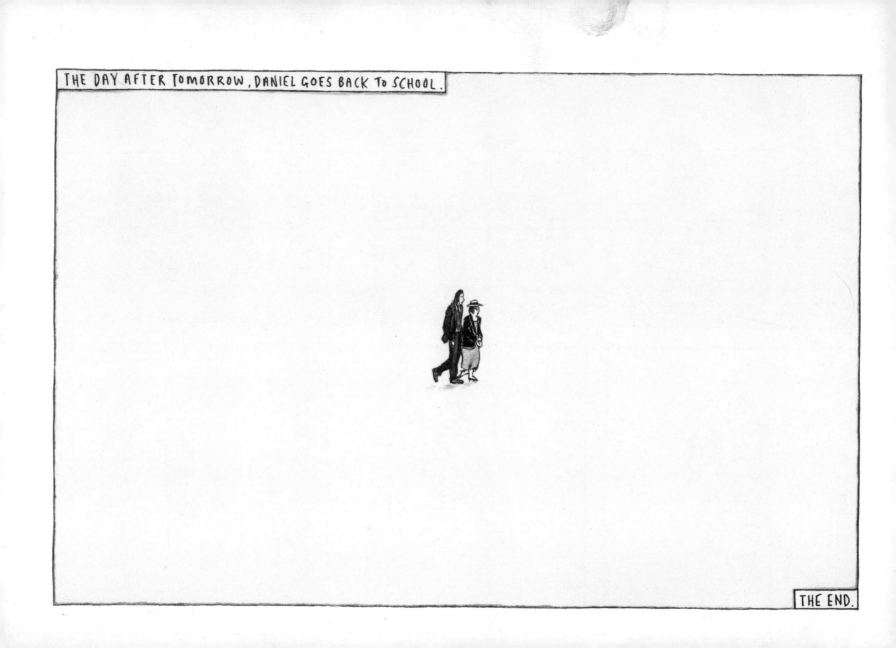

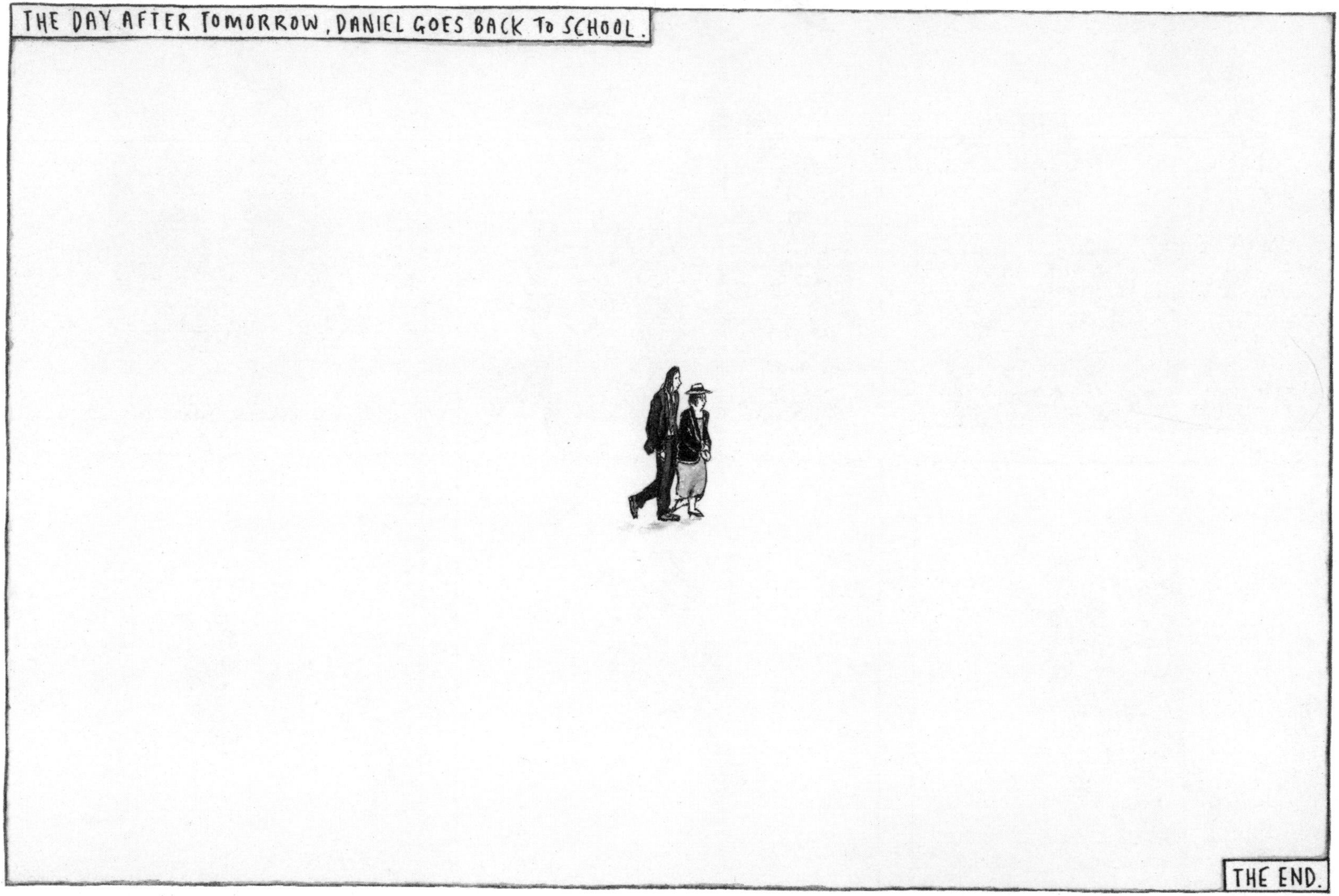
THE DAY AFTER TOMORROW, DANIEL GOES BACK TO SCHOOL.
THE END.